OUT & ABOUT

• WALKING GUIDES TO BRITAIN •

No 8

North Wales

From 1 April 1996, local authority boundaries in Wales will change.

For up-to-date information, contact the Local Government Reorganisation

Section of the Welsh Office on (01222) 825 111.

First published in Great Britain in 1996 by
Marshall Cavendish Books, London
(a division of Marshall Cavendish Partworks Ltd)

ISBN 0319 00579 8

British Library Cataloguing in Publication Data:
A catalogue record for this book is available from the British Library

Printed and bound in Malaysia

Some of this material has previously appeared in the Marshall Cavendish partwork OUT & ABOUT

While every effort has been made to check the accuracy of these walks, neither Marshall Cavendish nor Ordnance Survey can be held responsible for any errors or omissions, nor for any consequences arising from the use of information contained in this book. Marshall Cavendish welcomes readers' letters pointing out changes that have taken place in land ownership, access, etc., or inaccuracies in the walks' routes or descriptions.

Contents

Introduction to
OUT & ABOUT
• WALKING GUIDES TO BRITAIN •

Walking has become one of the most popular pastimes in Britain. To enjoy walking, you don't need any special skills, you don't have to follow rules or join expensive clubs, and you don't need any special equipment – though a pair of walking boots is a good idea! It is an easy way of relaxing and getting some exercise, and of enjoying nature and the changing seasons.

The OUT & ABOUT WALKING GUIDES TO BRITAIN will give you ideas for walks in your own neighbourhood and in other areas of Britain. All the walks are devised around a theme and range in length from about 2 to 9 miles (3.25 to 14.5 km) and in difficulty from very easy to mildly strenuous. Since each walk is circular, you will always be able to get back to your starting point.

Devised by experts and tested for accuracy, all the walks are accompanied by clear, practical instructions and an enlarged section of the relevant Ordnance Survey map. The flavour of the walk and highlights to look out for are described in the introductory text.

LOCAL COLOUR

Background features give you extra insight into items of local interest. The OUT & ABOUT WALKING GUIDES TO BRITAIN relate legends, point out unusual architectural details, provide a potted history of the lives of famous writers and artists connected with a particular place, explain traditional crafts still practised by local artisans, and uncover the secrets behind an ever-changing landscape.

DISCOVER NATURE

One of the greatest pleasures in going for a walk is the sense of being close to nature. On the walks suggested in the OUT & ABOUT WALKING GUIDES TO BRITAIN, you can feel the wind, smell the pine trees, hear the birds and see the beauty of the countryside. You will become more aware of the seasons – the life cycles of butterflies, the mating calls of birds, the protective behaviour of all creatures with their young. You will see the beginning of new life in the forests and fields, the bluebell carpets in spring woodlands, the dazzling beauty of rhododendron bushes in early summer, the swaying cornfields of summer and the golden colours of leaves in autumn. The OUT & ABOUT WALKING GUIDES TO BRITAIN tell you what to look out for and where to find it.

NATURE WALK

Occasional nature walk panels will highlight an interesting feature that you will see on your walk. You will learn about natural and manmade details in the landscape, how to tell which animal or bird has nibbled the cones in a pine forest, what nurse trees are and what a triangulation point is.

ABOVE: *Colourful narrowboats are always an attractive feature on inland waterways.*

FACT FILE

The fact file will give you at-a-glance information about each walk to help you make your selection.

- ✳ **general location**
- OS **map reference for Ordnance Survey map with grid reference for starting point**
- miles 0 1 2 3 4 5 6 7 8 9 / kms 0 1 2 3 4 5 6 7 8 9 10 11 12 13 14 15 **length of the walk in miles and kilometres**
- **time needed if walking at an average speed**
- **character of the walk: easy/easy with strenuous parts/mildly strenuous; hills to be climbed and muddy or dangerous areas are pointed out**
- P **parking facilities near the start of the walk**
- T **public transport information**
- **facilities for refreshment, including pubs serving lunchtime meals, restaurants, tea rooms and picnic areas**
- WC **location of toilets**
- **historic sites**

ORDNANCE SURVEY MAPS

All the walks in the OUT & ABOUT WALKING GUIDES TO BRITAIN are illustrated on large-scale, full-colour maps supplied by the Ordnance Survey. Ordnance Survey are justifiably proud of their worldwide reputation for excellence and accuracy. For extra clarity, the maps have been enlarged to a scale of 1:21,120 (3 inches to 1 mile).

The route for each walk is marked clearly on the map with a broken red line, and the numbers along the route refer you to the numbered stages in the written directions. In addition, points of interest are marked on the maps with letters. Each one is mentioned in the walk directions and is described in detail in the introductory text.

COUNTRYWISE

The countryside is one of our greatest resources. If we treat it with respect, we can preserve it for the future.

Throughout the countryside there is a network of paths and byways. Some are former trading routes, others are simply the paths villagers took to visit one another in the days before public transport. Most are designated 'rights of way': footpaths, open only to people on foot, and bridleways, open to people on foot, horseback or bicycle. These paths can be identified on Ordnance Survey maps and verified, in cases of dispute, by the definitive map for the area, held by the relevant local authority.

THE LAW OF TRESPASS

If you find a public right of way barred to you, you may remove the obstruction or take a short detour around it. However, in England and Wales, if you stray from the footpath you are trespassing and could be sued in a civil court for damages. In Scotland, rights of way are not recorded on definitive maps, nor is there a law of trespass. Although you may cross mountain and moorland paths, landowners are permitted to impose restrictions on access, such as during the grouse-shooting season, which should be obeyed.

If you are following a public right of way and find, for example, that your path is blocked by a field of crops, you are entitled to walk the line of the footpath through the crops, in single file. Farmers are required, by law, to restore public rights of way within 14 days of ploughing. However, if you feel uncomfortable about doing this and can find a way round, then do so. But report the matter to the local authority who will take the necessary action to clear the correct route.

RIGHT: *The stunning patchwork of fields surrounding the picturesque village of Widecombe in the heart of Dartmoor makes a beautiful setting for the famous annual fair.*
BELOW: *Brown hares boxing in spring are a fascinating sight.*

It is illegal for farmers to place a bull on its own in a field crossed by a right of way (unless the bull is not a recognized dairy breed). If you come across a bull alone in a field, find another way round.

COMMONS AND PARKS

There are certain areas in England and Wales where you may be able to wander without keeping to paths, such as most commons and beaches. There are also country parks, set up by local authorities for public recreation – parkland, woodland, heath or farmland.

The National Trust is the largest private landowner in England and Wales. Its purpose is to preserve areas of natural beauty and sites of historic interest by acquisition, holding them in trust for public access and enjoyment. Information on access may be obtained from National Trust headquarters at

THE COUNTRY CODE

- Enjoy the countryside, and respect its life and work
- Always guard against risk of fire
- Fasten all gates
- Keep your dogs under close control
- Keep to public footpaths across farmland
- Use gates and stiles to cross fences, hedges and walls
- Leave livestock, crops and machinery alone
- Take your litter home
- Help to keep all water clean
- Protect wildlife, plants and trees
- Take special care on country roads
- Make no unnecessary noise

36 QueenAnne's Gate, London SW1H 9AS
Tel: 0171-222 9251.

Most regions of great scenic beauty in England and Wales are designated National Parks or Areas of Outstanding Natural Beauty (AONB). In Scotland, they are known as National Scenic Areas (NSAs) or AONBs.

Most of this land is privately owned and there is no right of public access. In some cases, local authorities may have negotiated agreements with landowners to allow walkers access on mountains and moors.

CONSERVATION

National park, AONB or NSA status is intended to provide some measure of protection for the land-scape, guarding against unsuitable development while encouraging enjoyment of its natural beauty.

ABOVE RIGHT *Carelessness with cigarettes, matches or camp fires can be devastating in a forest.*

Nature reserves are areas set aside for conservation. Most are privately owned, some by large organizations such as the Royal Society for the Protection of Birds. Although some offer public access, most require permission to enter.

THE RAMBLERS ASSOCIATION

The aims of the Ramblers Association are to further greater understanding and care of the countryside, to protect and enhance public rights of way and areas of natural beauty, to improve public access to the countryside, and to encourage more people to take up rambling as a healthy, recreational activity. It has played an important role in preserving and developing our national footpath network.

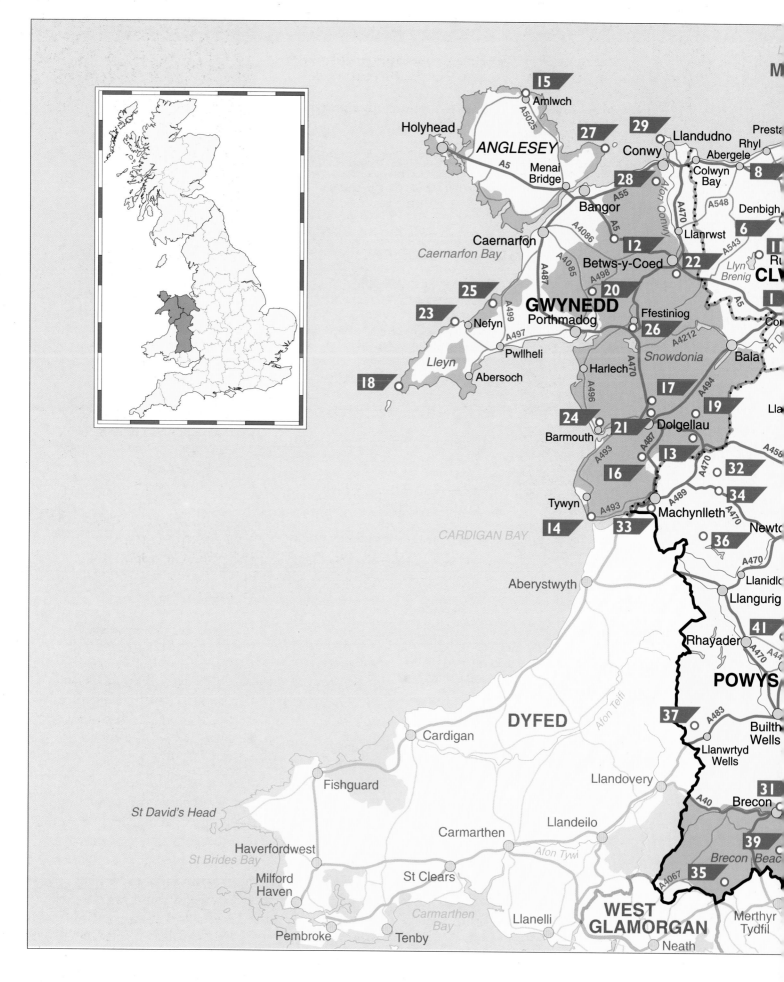

North Wales

All the walks featured in this book are plotted and numbered on the regional map (left) and listed in the box below.

USING MAPS

Although the OUT & ABOUT WALKING GUIDES TO BRITAIN give you all the information you need, it is useful to have some basic map skills. Most of us have some experience of using a motoring atlas to navigate by car. Navigating when walking is much the same, except that mistakes are much more time and energy consuming and, if circumstances conspire, could lead to an accident.

A large-scale map is the answer to identifying where you are. Britain is fortunate in having the best mapping agency in the world, the Ordnance Survey, which produces high-quality maps, the most popular being the 1:50,000 Landranger series. However, the most useful for walkers are the 1:25,000 Pathfinder, Explorer and Outdoor Leisure maps.

THE LIE OF THE LAND

A map provides more than just a bird's eye view of the land; it also conveys information about the terrain – whether marshy, forested, covered with tussocky grass or boulders; it distinguishes between footpaths and bridleways; and shows boundaries such as parish and county boundaries.

Symbols are used to identify a variety of land-marks such as churches, camp and caravan sites, bus, coach and rail stations, castles, caves and historic houses. Perhaps most importantly of all, the shape of the land is indicated by contour lines. Each line represents land at a specific height so it is possible to read the gradient from the spacing of the lines (the closer the spacing, the steeper the hill).

GRID REFERENCES

All Ordnance Survey maps are over-printed with a framework of squares known as the National Grid. This is a reference system which, by breaking the country down into squares, allows you to pinpoint any place in the country and give it a unique reference number; very useful when making rendezvous arrangements. On OS Landranger, Pathfinder and Outdoor Leisure maps it is possible to give a reference to an accuarcy of 100 metres. Grid squares on these maps cover an area of 1 km x 1 km on the ground.

GIVING A GRID REFERENCE

Blenheim Palace in Oxfordshire has a grid reference of **SP 441 161.** This is constructed as follows:

SP These letters identify the 100 km grid square in which Blenheim Palace lies. These squares form the basis of the National Grid. Information on the

100 km square covering a particular map is always given in the map key.

441 161 This six figure reference locates the position of Blenheim Palace to 100 metres in the 100 km grid square.

44 This part of the reference is the number of the grid line which forms the western (left-hand) boundary of the 1 km grid square in which Blenheim Palace appears. This number is printed in the top and bottom margins of the relevant OS map (Pathfinder 1092 in this case).

16 This part of the reference is the number of the grid line which forms the southern (lower) boundary of the 1 km grid square in which Blenheim Palace appears. This number is printed in the left- and right-hand margins of the relevant OS map (Pathfinder 1092).

These two numbers together (SP 4416) locate the bottom left-hand corner of

the 1 km grid square in which Blenheim Palace appears. The remaining figures in the reference **441 161** pinpoint the position within that square by dividing its western boundary lines into tenths and estimating on which imaginary tenths line Blenheim Palace lies.

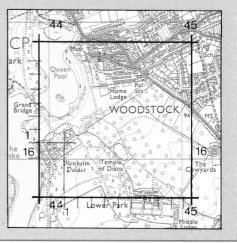

DOWN THE DEE VALLEY

Through wood and valley to an ancient hill site

Variety is the essence of this walk. The path starts from the centre of a small town, then climbs to the mixed woodland of Coed Pen-y-pigyn from where there is an impressive view of the Dee valley. Descending to the valley floor, the walk continues along a gentle riverside path beside the River Dee.

An additional diversion is the steep ascent along unofficial but well-used paths to the 960 foot (294 metre) summit of Caer Drewyn. Here are the remains of an ancient hill fortress where once the Welsh gathered forces against the English.

Corwen is a busy little market town at the foot of the Berwyns. The Church of St Mael and St Sulien **A** in part dates back to the 13th century. It is dedicated to two 6th-century Celtic saints. A 9th-century cross-shaft stands outside its south-west corner.

A STONE CIRCLE

There is nothing ancient about the circle of standing stones in the forest clearing **B**, although the native broad-leaved trees give a feeling of antiquity. This is a Gorsedd circle, one of many erected near

▲ *The bridge over the River Dee at Corwen. (inset) The bright golden-ringed dragonfly feeds on insects, often on the wing.*

▼ *The medieval Church of St Mael and St Sulien at the start of the walk.*

places where the Royal National Eisteddfod has been held. The stones are the setting for ceremonies derived from ancient practices, and were first used in 1919.

View of the Dee valley towards Llangollen from the Pen-y-pigyn lookout point.

FACT FILE

- ☀ Corwen, Clwyd 8 miles (13 km) west of Llangollen on A5

- 🗺 Pathfinder 805 (SJ 04/14), grid reference SJ 078434

  miles 0 1 2 3 4 5 6 7 8 9 10 miles
  kms 0 1 2 3 4 5 6 7 8 9 10 11 12 13 14 15 kms

- ◔ Allow 2½ hours with 40 minutes extra for the optional ascent of Caer Drewyn

- ▰ Steep in places and could be muddy by the river. Walking shoes recommended

- 🅿 Car park signposted off the A5 in the centre of Corwen (up Y Lon Las)

- 🚌 Corwen is served by buses from Wrexham (D94), Barmouth (D94) and Rhyl (N51)

- 🍴 All facilities in Corwen

- 🚻 At car park

The woodlands of Coed Pen-y-pigyn contain sessile oak, rowan (mountain ash) and silver birch. There are also plantations of conifers. From here, the viewpoint **C** overlooks the town and the Dee valley. A cone-shaped memorial surmounted by a flagpole commemorates the marriage of the Prince of Wales (King Edward VII) with Princess Alexandra of Denmark in 1863, and the investiture of Edward Prince of Wales (later Duke of Windsor) in 1911.

THE WALK

CORWEN - CAER DREWYN

The walk begins at the front of the Eagles Hotel in the centre of Corwen.

▶**1** With your back to the hotel, go right towards the traffic lights. Just before them, turn left through the lychgate to the Church of St Mael and St Sulien **Ⓐ**. Go right to leave the churchyard by a turnstile and bear left up a lane.

▶**2** The lane soon becomes a path that climbs between walls from one gate to another. Entering the forest, keep going uphill and bear right to a stone circle in a clearing **Ⓑ**. Do not go through the metal gate, but resume the uphill path which veers left. Ascend steps with a wall on your right and pass through a gap in it to reach a viewpoint **Ⓒ**.

▶**3** Turn sharply right to take a path from the back of the viewpoint to a forest track. Go right, crossing a stile beside a gate ahead, to reach a footpath signpost at a track junction. Turn right to walk 400 yards (360 metres) to a bridleway signpost.

▶**4** Fork right downhill and through a wooden gate. Descend past a

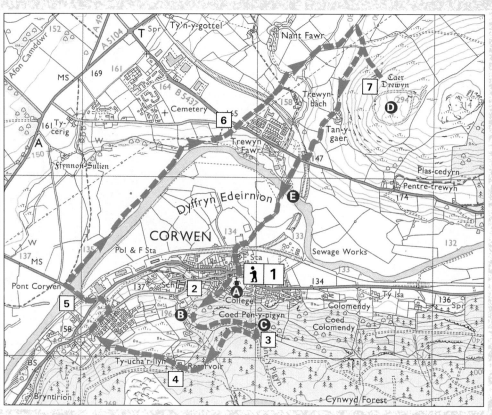

reservoir and a house and go ahead through a gate to reach a junction. Turn right for 250 yards (225 metres) then take a signposted path on your left down steps to the A5 near its junction with the B4401. Cross the road carefully and bear left along the A5 towards Bala.

▶**5** Cross the bridge over the River Dee (no footway) and turn right along the riverside path, with the Dee on your right. After leaving the meadow, go ahead over a

footbridge and follow the path, keeping right and following the bend of the river. Go up steps to a stile. Maintain this direction across a second field, then turn left uphill across the third field to a signposted stile beside a gate.

▶**6** Go ahead across a road and up a metalled minor road. Ignore the first turning on your right, but take the second (a hedged track) to a stile beside a gate, with Caer Drewyn facing you. The

track continues beside the hedge on your right, but you may wish to go up the steep hill to see the Iron Age hill fort **Ⓓ**.

▶**7** Return to the track and walk with the hedge on your right. Go over a stile beside a gate ahead, to fork right past a farm on your left down to a road. Go right at a junction, then left towards Corwen. Cross the River Dee **Ⓔ** and pass the site of the old railway station on your way back to the starting point.

On Caer Drewyn **Ⓓ** is an Iron Age hillfort. This is where Owain Gwynedd mustered his Welsh army in response to King Henry II's invasion of Wales in 1164. However, Henry retreated due to bad weather conditions, but not before putting out the eyes of his Welsh hostages, including two of Owain's sons.

Ramparts of the Iron Age hillfort on top of Caer Drewyn.

In the middle of the River Dee **Ⓔ** stands a lone pillar which was once part of an old railway bridge. This used to support the Denbigh, Ruthin & Corwen Railway. Opened in 1864, this railway was joined at Corwen by a line from Ruabon in 1865 that was to reach Barmouth in 1869. Corwen then became an important station, with waiting rooms, refreshments and sidings. Sadly, trains ceased running in 1965.

A woodland walk past lakes in a valley fed by a holy spring

Nature has returned in triumph to reclaim the Greenfield Valley, but there is plenty here to give delight to all interested in our heritage from the Industrial Revolution. Oak trees now enclose the track of the old, dismantled railway, but a succession of lakes can be glimpsed. The lakes are artificial reservoirs built to provide power for the mills. Copper and cotton made this valley prosperous during the 19th century. However, the industries declined and later departed. Still here, though, is the most famous holy well or spring in Wales.

PILGRIMS' PROGRESS

The walk down Well Street is a journey in time from a modern, bustling town to an age of faith and miracles. The vast numbers who make it testify to the reputation of St Winefride's holy well **A** as 'the Lourdes of Wales'. One of the 'Seven Wonders of Wales', it is renowned for curing nervous disorders.

St Winefride, or Gwenffrewi in Welsh, after whom the well is named, lived in the 7th century and was the daughter of a local chief. Her mother, Gwenlo, was the sister

Legend says the holy spring bubbled up where Winefride's severed head landed.

of St Beune, who instructed her in the Christian faith. Her uncle also gained a reputation for restoring to life people who had 'lost their heads'. Legend has it that their heads were cut off and he put them back. The miracle may have been that the saint helped them to recover their sanity. So it was with his niece, Winefride. Caradog, the chieftain of Hawarden, frightened her and 'cut off her head'; Beune restored it and made Caradog 'melt away'.

The severed head was credited with landing where the holy well, or spring, is now. Winefride became a nun, then went to Gwytherin in Denbighshire to be the abbess of a convent. Regular services are held and the tradition is for pilgrims to pass through the water three times. Henry V came here in 1415 before the Battle of Agincourt, while James II and Queen Mary prayed (successfully) for a son in 1686.

The Holywell Textile Company has a shop here **B**. Although the high-quality fabrics are no longer

▲ *St Winefride's Well is the 'Lourdes of Wales' and for centuries pilgrims have sought the restorative powers of its waters. The flowers of the wood anemone (inset) open when it is sunny.*

FACT FILE

✳	Holywell, Clwyd
🚉	Pathfinder 755 (SJ 07/17), grid reference SJ 185759

miles 0 1 2 3 4 5 6 7 8 9 10 miles
kms 0 1 2 3 4 5 6 7 8 9 10 11 12 13 14 15 kms

◔	Allow 1½ hours
▭	Easy; good, firm, level tracks
P	Car parks in Holywell, including at the start of walk
🍴	Pubs and restaurants in Holywell
🏛	St Winefride's Well open Tues-Sun; Abbey Farm and Visitor Centre open daily, April-October and sometimes at weekends during the winter

THE WALK

HOLYWELL AND THE GREENFIELD VALLEY

The walk begins at the top of Well Street, Holywell. There is a car park here; while other car parks are near the bus stand 250 yards (225 metres) away. Buses come from Rhyl and Chester (nos X2, A6, A7, A8, A9 and A18). Well Street is clearly marked.

1 ▶ Go down Well Street, passing Plas Dewi on your left. Continue downhill to a Protestant church and a Roman Catholic chapel above St Winefride's holy well **A**. Go left to the road, then right along the pavement past the entrance to the holy well, the Textile Mill's shop **B** and Hall's Drinks factory to the Royal Oak Inn, on your right.

2 ▶ Turn right, then almost immediately left to walk past a lake on your right.

3 ▶ Turn right to pass above the Battery Works **C** on your left. Go ahead past

a chimney into woodland.

4 ▶ Turn left along the track of a dismantled railway **D** . Pass another lake on your left. Reach a track junction where your way lies ahead, on the level track. First, however, divert uphill on your right to see part of Wat's Dyke **E** on your left. Resume your former direction along the old railway track. Pass a third lake on your left. Keep to the level track ahead at the next junction.

5 ▶ Follow the track across a footbridge, then bear left down steps to the ruins of Basingwerk Abbey **F** . Go left, past the abbey and Basingwerk House on your right. Pass the Abbey Farm Museum and Visitor Centre **G** on your left.

6 ▶ Go left to pass the ruins of the Abbey Wire Mill **H**, the Victoria Mill **J** and a lake on your right. Return to the old railway and follow it past the ruins

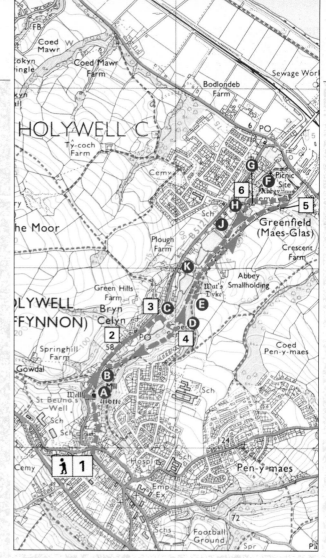

of Meadow Mill **K** and three more lakes on your right. Fork right as signposted to St Winefride's Halt. Bear right to the road and go left back to the start.

---

made in Holywell, this company is descended from the Welsh Flannel Company, established in 1874.

HIVE OF INDUSTRY

The Battery Works **C** were built in 1766 and pots and pans were made from brass sheets. The finished goods were exported to Africa, where they were traded for slaves.

The dismantled railway **D** began life in 1869 as a link between the town of Holywell and its port at Greenfield, on the Dee Estuary. It was soon abandoned, only to be developed in 1912 as a branch of the main Chester-Holyhead line. Before its closure in 1954, its little train steamed up a 1:27 gradient.

Wat's Dyke **E** predates Offa's Dyke, having been built by his predecessor, Ethelbald, who ruled Mercia from 725 to 757. This border earthwork between the Welsh and the Mercians ran from Holywell to south of Oswestry.

Basingwerk Abbey **F** was founded by the Cistercians in 1132. The monks built the first water mills in this valley— to grind corn and a fulling mill to process the wool from the sheep they introduced.

The Abbey Farm Museum and Visitor Centre **G** is well worth a

◀ Basingwerk Abbey fell into ruin after the Dissolution of the monasteries in 1536. Wat's Dyke (right) kept the Welsh at bay.

visit. The farm buildings have been reconstructed from different periods. Copper and brass wire were once made at the Abbey Wire Mill **H**.

A large water-wheel-powered Victoria Mill **J** was built in 1785 as a cotton mill but later used as a corn mill. Rolled copper sheets were once produced at Meadow Mill **K** .

LLANTYSILIO MOUNTAIN

Where an 'eagle' fell to earth on Moel y Gaer hillfort

Moel y Gaer literally means 'fort on a bare hill'. Ascending to a height of 1,655 feet (504 metres) might seem forbidding, but this walk is well within nearly everybody's capabilities and can only be described as a moderate climb. Since Rhewl, at the beginning of this walk, lies at a height of 400 feet (120 metres) the actual ascent is only 1,250 feet (384 metres). In addition, the paths on this walk are good and offer easy access to the top of the hill.

SUPERB VIEWS

The climb up to Moel y Gaer affords real mountain views — over the Berwyns to the south and the Clwyd Mountains to the north — that deserve a clear day to be appreciated. The heather- and bracken-covered hills are magnificent. Although the aspect can sometimes be stark because of the lack of trees, the valleys are clad in deciduous

▲Bwlch-y-garnedd cottage nestles in the valley below Moel y Gaer. The polecat (right) was once called the foulmart because of its strong smell. It faced extinction because it was trapped extensively for its fur, known as fitch.

FACT FILE

⊛ Llantysilio Mountain, Rhewl, Clwyd. Off the A5, 3 miles (5 km) west of Llangollen

▭▭ Pathfinder 805 (SJ 04/14), grid reference SJ 179447

miles 0 1 2 3 4 5 6 7 8 9 10 miles
kms 0 1 2 3 4 5 6 7 8 9 10 11 12 13 14 15 kms

◖ Allow 2½ hours

◼ Moderate climb along good paths. Walking shoes are recommended

P You are welcome to park opposite the Sun Inn, Rhewl, but please note that there is more space in the mornings at the weekends

🍴 Sun Inn at start of walk and the Conquering Hero, Rhewl

woodland and the conifer plantations support a variety of wildlife.

The hamlet of Rhewl lies on the edge of the River Dee, or Afon Dyfrdwy, which flows from Llyn Tegid at Bala to its estuary just north of Chester. Llyn Tegid lies about 12 miles (19 km) to the west. It is the largest natural lake in Wales and rich in a wide variety of fish.

Llantysilio Mountain, just north of the rugged Berwyn Hills, lies in the heart of Owain Glyndwr country. The legendary Welsh hero took his name from the nearby village of Glyndyfrdwy — he was lord of Sycarth and Glyndyfrdwy. Not far away is Glyndwr's Mount, the site of one of his halls, where the sustained Welsh revolt against the oppressive English began on 16th September 1400 and Glyndwr was proclaimed Prince of Wales.

Talk to the locals at the Sun Inn Ⓐ, the 14th-century drovers' inn at the start of this walk in Rhewl, and some may remember the tragedy that happened on Moel y Gaer in 1942. The event has given this hill a new name — Moel y Dakota.

Starting at Rhewl, the walk leads up hedge-lined tracks until you reach Bwlch-y-garnedd Ⓑ, a cottage in the valley, encircled by the purple and russet mountains. It was the home of Harry Roberts, a shepherd.

OUT OF THE BLUE

In August, 1942, he was enjoying a quiet, after-lunch stroll around the fields when there was the sound of an aircraft crashing on Moel y Gaer — confirmed by an engine bouncing down the cliff to land in some nearby trees. Taking the narrow path to the top, Harry Roberts met an airman stumbling down the hill. Using uprooted heather to beat out the flames that engulfed him, Harry sat the airman on a rock beside the path

THE WALK

RHEWL – MOEL Y GAER

The walk begins from the Sun Inn, Rhewl, off the A5 about 3 miles (4.8 km) west of Llangollen.

▶ Facing the Sun Inn **A**, go right, then left up a lane marked 'No Through Road'. Pass a track on your left and a white cottage (Bryn Melyn).

▶ Bear left at the next fork to take the lower track. Go around a hairpin bend and through a gate across the track. Go ahead 200 yards (180 metres).

▶ Turn right up a hedged track. Continue through a gate and, with a fence on your right, go past an old quarry spoil on your left. Reach Bwlch-y-garnedd cottage **B**.

▶ Pass the cottage on your right and take a gate to the left of a farm building ahead. Cross a brook and walk beside a fence with a conifer plantation behind it on your left. Cross a stile in a fixed gate at the end of this enclosed path.

▶ Walk beside a fence on your right for 20 yards (18 metres), then veer slightly left along a path that gradually ascends through the bracken. Continue up a narrow path to a gate in the top fence with a stile to the left of it.

▶ Go ahead over the stile to reach a green track. Turn left along this to the summit of Moel y Gaer **C**.

▶ After admiring the view, retrace your steps along the green track to a crosstracks in the pass leading between Moel y Gaer and Moel Gamelin.

▶ Turn right along the track but veer right from it as it approaches a fence. Go ahead over a stile in the fence and descend, with another fence on your right. Go ahead, descending gradually with the path while the fence bears right more steeply down the valley. When the fence climbs back to meet the path again, walk with it on your right. Ignore a stile in the fence on your right, but cross a stile ahead and follow the path to a conifer plantation.

▶ Fork right to cross a stile and descend, with conifer trees on your right. Go ahead through a gate and below a house on your left. Continue down the steep track, which passes above a farmhouse (Cae-Llewelyn) on your right. Go down a hedged lane to return to the Sun Inn.

◀ *A view of the russet-coloured hills looking back along the hedge-lined lane above an isolated farmhouse.*

and entered the mist to reach the summit. The rocky summit of Moel y Gaer hillfort **C** — one of the highest Iron Age settlements in Britain — was strewn with blazing wreckage. The wing tip of the C47 Skytrain, more commonly known as a Dakota, had clipped the rampart of the hillfort. Thanks to the shepherd's prompt action at effecting a rescue, the airman survived. The other 11 crew and passengers died.

Walkers on Moel y Gaer today are unlikely to have the quiet of the mountain shattered by such a dramatic landing. However, take care if you visit the area in the autumn or the peace may be interrupted by a more sinister character. Blackberries abound near the end of the walk, but do not pick them after September for legend has it that they then belong to the Devil, who guards them jealously!

BIRDS OF PREY

Even in spring and summer, birdlife can be sparse on the hills, but look out for buzzards circling in the sky above, and kestrels and sparrowhawks hovering, ready to swoop on unsuspecting prey.

CLWYD

from Ruabon to Dolgellau. It received its first train in 1862 and the line westward to Corwen opened in 1865, just a century before British Rail closed this route. Preservationists reopened the station in 1975 and the Llangollen Railway Society now runs steam trains to Carrog.

The limestone escarpment of Trevor Rocks **C** is an impressive sight. It began as a coral reef in

◄ *Castell Dinas Bran commands a spectacular view of the surrounding countryside. The strong odour of herb Robert (below) has earned the plant the nickname of 'Stinking Bob'.*

Above Llangollen and past the ruins of a 13th-century Cistercian abbey

Limestone cliffs, a stiff climb up the grassy slopes of a conical hill and the tranquillity of a canal tow path combine to make this a varied walk. Although it is rich in

legend, history and culture, nature is not to be outdone. Come in spring to see alder catkins hanging from the trees, or enjoy a summer ramble with the company of lime-loving, common blue butterflies.

Llangollen is the sacred enclosure of St Collen, who made his name in the 7th century for dealing with fairies. It is the bridge **A** that finds its way into the old rhyme about the seven wonders of Wales, however.

SPANNING THE YEARS

Originally a pack-horse bridge, built by John Trevor, Bishop of St Asaph, in 1345, it has been widened several times since. The rapids below it are a testing ground for canoeists.

Llangollen Railway Station **B** was on the Great Western Railway's line

◄*Llangollen's charming 14th-century pack-horse bridge, which spans the rapids of the River Dee, is one of the seven wonders of Wales.*

FACT FILE

✳ Llangollen, Clwyd

▱ Pathfinder 806, (SJ 24/34), grid reference SJ 214419

miles 0 1 2 3 4 5 6 7 8 9 10 miles
kms 0 1 2 3 4 5 6 7 8 9 10 11 12 13 14 15 kms

◗ Allow 3½ hours

▬ Moderate, with one strenuous climb and an easy final section. Good walking shoes are recommended for climbing Castell Dinas Bran

P In Llangollen, between the A5 and Market Street

T Bus 94 between Barmouth and Wrexham

A variety of pubs, cafés, restaurants and shops available in Llangollen

THE WALK

THE VALE OF LLANGOLLEN

The walk begins from the Tourist Information Centre in Castle Street, Llangollen, just off the A5.

1 Go left down Castle Street and across Bishop Trevor Bridge **A** over the River Dee. Llangollen Railway Station **B** is on your left. Turn right for about 20 yards (18 metres), then turn left up Wharf Hill. Cross a bridge over the Llangollen Canal.

2 Go straight ahead up the path signposted 'Castell Dinas Bran', passing a school on your left. The fenced path ends at a gate. Go ahead, as signposted, uphill. Continue through a small gate in the top corner to follow a hedged track to a crosstrack.

3 Turn right to follow a track to a gate. Continue along the top of two fields, keeping a fence on your left, until you arrive at a tarmac lane.

4 Go ahead across the lane and over a stile in the fence to the left of the gateway to Wern-uchaf. Continue through a gate in the next corner and veer left across a field to a stile. Cross it and turn left immediately to go over a stile beside a gate and descend with a fence on your right. Turn right with this fence, as signposted, continue over a stile beside a gate and descend to another stile.

5 Cross the stile, ignore a gate on your left immediately after it and veer left to cross a stile beside a gate. Climb to a stile beside a gate and a signpost and follow a track at the foot of trees for 100 yards (90 metres), where it forks. Ignore the uphill track by going ahead over a stile beside a gate and a signpost. Maintain your height across the fields, then eventually bear uphill to a gate which gives access to a lane.

6 Turn left up the lane to a road. Turn left along this, soon joining the Panorama Road below Trevor Rocks **C** on your right. Pass the acorn signpost of the Offa's Dyke Path, then ignore a signposted footpath on your left.

7 Turn left over a cattle grid and follow a lane for 100 yards (90 metres). Veer right over a signposted stile and climb the waymarked path up to Castell Dinas Bran **D**. Descend along the waymarked zigzag path on the other side of the hill, overlooking the town of Llangollen.

8 Join a path running beside the bottom fence on your right and turn right along it, with the fence on your left. Reach a signpost and turn left over a stile. Descend with a fence on your right to a stile beside a gate. Cross this and turn right up a road. Pass Dinbren Road on your right and reach the B5103. Go right for approximately 150 yards (135 metres).

9 As the road bears left, go straight ahead over the stile beside a gate. Follow the track beside a hedge on your right through two gates, then cut across the corner of a field to a signpost above woodland.

Descend through trees and above a stream on the left.

10 Turn left across a footbridge. Pass the ruins of Valle Crucis Abbey **E** on your left, then bear right up its access road. Keep right along the A542 for 300 yards (270 metres) to see Eliseg's Pillar **F** in a field on your right.

11 Return along the main road, taking the elevated pavement on its right-hand side as you pass above the abbey on your left. Ignore the B5103 going to Corwen on your right and go ahead to walk with the canal on your right and turn right when you reach a bridge across it.

12 Turn left to join the tow path and walk with the canal on your left. Pass the Llangollen Railway on your right, go under a road bridge and continue under the old canal bridge no. 46. Pass the grounds of the International Eisteddfod **G** on your right, reach the Canal Exhibition **H** at Llangollen Wharf and bear right to retrace your steps to the start of the walk.

▲ *The River Dee snakes its way through the beautiful Vale of Llangollen accompanied by the Llangollen Canal, a branch of the Shropshire Union.*

▶ *The Llangollen Railway Society reopened the station in 1975 and runs trains to Carrog, 8 miles (13km) away.*

tropical water 350 million years ago. The Offa's Dyke Path follows this road on its journey of some 170 miles (273 km) between Chepstow and Prestatyn, although the nearest stretch of dyke is actually the earlier Wat's Dyke, about 6 miles (9.6 km) to the east.

VALLEY VIEWS

There are splendid views all along this walk, but the best are seen from Castell Dinas Bran **D**. Descending into the valley, the path leads to the ruins of Valle Crucis Abbey **E**. It was actually dedicated to St Mary, while the cross referred to in the

valley's name is the nearby Pillar of Eliseg **F**. The abbey was endowed by Madoc ap Grufydd, Prince of Powys Fadog (or North Powys), on 28th January, 1201.

Its first monks came from Strata Marcella near Welshpool and were

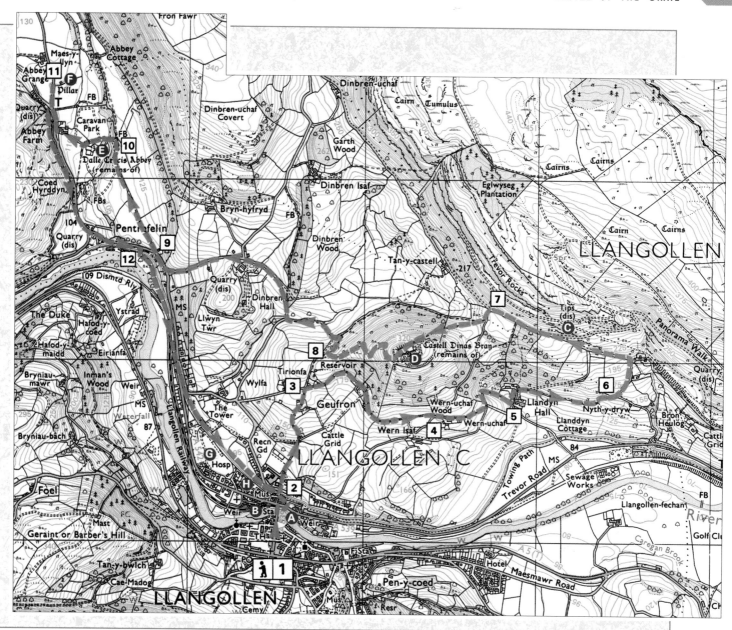

Cistercians, renowned for their hard work and self-sufficiency. Its resulting prosperity was affected by the Welsh wars, but it was peaceful and wealthy in the early 14th century.

The Black Death of 1349 was followed by Owain Glyndwr's fight for liberation, however. An old story tells of the abbot of Valle Crucis meeting his neighbour Owain Glyndwr while taking an early morning stroll by the River Dee. Owain joked that the abbot was up early, but the abbot replied that it was Owain who had risen too soon — a century too soon. This was a prophecy of Henry Tudor's victory at the Battle of Bosworth in 1485. The Tudors were later to dissolve the abbeys but the number of monks had dwindled in number

and had lapsed from the strict Cistercian rules by the time Valle Crucis was closed in 1537 after the Dissolution of the Monasteries. Its ruins are in the care of CADW (Welsh Historic Monuments).

BROKEN CROSS

The Pillar of Eliseg now stands 8 feet (2.4 metres) high. It was broken during the Civil War and originally formed a cross of about 20 feet (6.1 metres) in height. This is the cross that gave its name to this valley and would seem to mark the crossing point of male and female earth energy lines (the Michael and Mary lines). Its significance led to a man (possibly Eliseg) being buried here, under the cross. The tumulus was opened up before the pillar was

▼*Not Welsh national dress, but colourful Turkish singers and dancers at the International Musical Eisteddfod.*

Castell Dinas Bran

This conical hill rises to 1,062 feet (324 metres) above sea level. Its shape resembles Glastonbury Tor and both places are associated with St Collen and the fairies, whom he made vanish with a sprinkling of holy water. The castle is linked with the legend of the holy grail.

Bran is Bron, the king who features in the Arthurian legends, and his castle was visited by Sir Perceval. Bran the Blessed was also a famous British king. The ruined castle on the summit was not built until the 13th century but it occupies a corner of an old hillfort that probably dates back to the Bronze Age. An earlier wooden castle may well have been burnt down.

But what of the grail? The grail story is viewed as a parable, rather than a factual story about a physical cup used by Christ at the Last Supper. Dowsing has shown that Glastonbury Tor has a current of female (Mary) energy forming a container (cup) shape around its summit. Male (Michael) energy can be dowsed forming a three-dimensional maze around the hill, culminating in a long stem with a bulbous head penetrating, or being enclosed by, the double-lipped cup of the Mary energies. Here we have the union of the earth's male and female energies.

It would seem that Castell Dinas Bran conforms to the same pattern. It could well be that the earliest earthworks on Castell Dinas Bran were for religious rather than

defensive purposes at a time when the earth was respected as a living being. The site was too good to be missed by Gruffydd ap Madoc when he needed a

stone castle in the 13th century. As a supporter of the English king Henry III, and the husband of an Englishwoman, he needed the protection from his own subjects.

The castle was in Welsh hands when Edward I invaded in 1277, but Llywelyn the Last's men chose to vacate and burn it as they retreated from the English advance. It was never repaired, although the beautiful Myfanwy Fychan resided here in the 14th century. Her admirer, the poet

Hywel ap Einion, wrote his verses in praise of her ('fair as the driven snow on the Arans') in an oak tree on the slope of this hill. The haunting melody

The old French name for the Castle of the Grail was Corbenic, which is derived from corbin, meaning raven or crow and Castell Dinas Bran means 'Crow Castle' in Welsh.

'Myfanwy' is a memorial to this unrequited love.

By 1490, when Leland came this way, the castle's only inhabitant was a fierce eagle. A golden harp is said to be hidden in the hill. According to legend, it can only be found by a boy and a white dog with a silver eye.

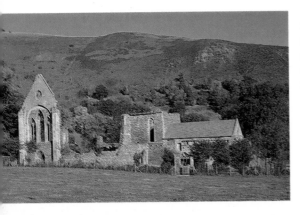

▲ *The ruins of the Cistercian Valle Crucis Abbey house an exhibition on monastic life until the Dissolution in 1535.*

re-erected in 1779. It was found to contain the skeleton of a man plus a silver coin, which would rule out an early date to his burial. The pillar is most famous for its Latin inscription. This is now indecipherable, but it was carefully transcribed by Edward Lhuyd in 1696. The 31 lines of Latin record that the stone was erected by Concenn, great-grandson of Eliseg, who fought to save Powys from the English.

Come in early July to have a look at the tented pavilion on the grounds of the Llangollen International Eisteddfod ❻. Since 1947 this annual event has attracted

singers, dancers and musicians from all over the world. The feast of colours is especially vivid on the Wednesday, when folk dancers take the stage and can be seen practising beforehand in the grounds or around the town.

Celebrate the end of this walk with a leisurely cruise in a horse-drawn barge. This starts from Llangollen Wharf, where there is an excellent Canal Exhibition ❽. Notice the crane that has been carefully preserved outside. The Llangollen Canal is a branch of the Shropshire Union Canal and was completed in 1805 by Thomas Telford.

Through a canal tunnel and over an aqueduct via Chirk Castle

Shropshire may form part of England now but it was Welsh until the 8th century and in Wales it is considered to be a 'lost territory'. This walk crosses the border with the canal and its towpath is a very easy route. The former strategic nature of the border area is reflected in its castles, but peace now reigns in this beautiful river valley.

Horse-drawn trams once pulled trucks of slate here and the line's promoter spotted its potential as a tourist attraction. The tracks have gone, but it remains popular with walkers, at its junction with Offa's Dyke Path and the Maelor Way.

The Industrial Revolution led to the construction of transport routes to open up the mineral wealth of this area. One of these was the quaint little Glyn Valley Tramway (GVT). This used to go under the second of the two bridges **A** at Chirk

FACT FILE

* Chirk, 5 miles (8 km) north of Oswestry

* Pathfinder 827 (SJ 23/33), grid reference SJ 285378

  miles 0 1 2 3 4 5 6 7 8 9 10 miles
  kms 0 1 2 3 4 5 6 7 8 9 10 11 12 13 14 15 kms

* 3½ hours; extra to visit castle

* Along towpaths, through fields and woods. Take a torch for the tunnel

* **P** At Chirk station at the start

* **T** Trains from Chester and Shrewsbury; Crosville buses 2 (Wrexham–Shrewsbury) and 2A (Wrexham–Oswestry)

* Chirk Castle is open from Easter–end September, and at weekends in October. For opening times, Tel. (01691) 777701

* **I** Part of the walk is on a courtesy path, which is only open from Easter–September

▲*Originally planned to link up the rivers Severn and Mersey, the Llangollen Canal today is a popular thoroughfare for leisure craft. The pond skater (inset) feeds on insects.*

Station, where it terminated. The GVT followed the River Ceiriog for 9 miles (14 km) between Glyn Ceiriog and Chirk. Its original gauge was 2 feet 4 ¼ inches (0.72 metres)

▼*Viaducts such as this one used to carry the many new railway lines born out of the Industrial Revolution.*

THE WALK

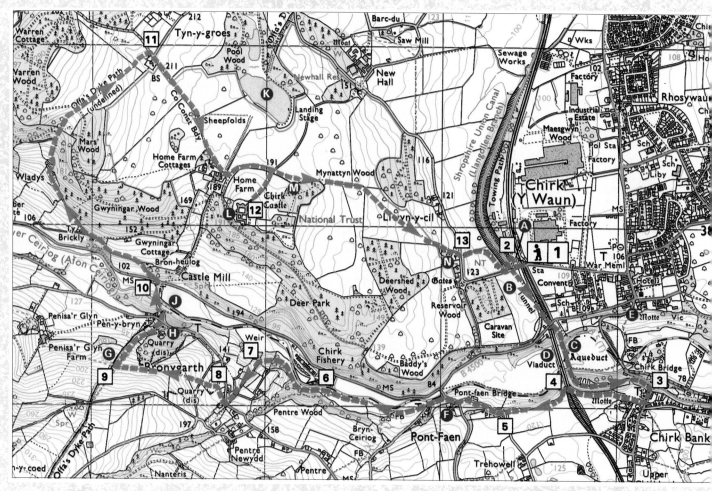

CHIRK CASTLE AND CANAL

The walk begins at Chirk's British Rail station. (Note: This walk can only be completed when Chirk Castle is open — see Fact File.)

1 Go right across what are actually two bridges **A**. Pass an industrial estate road on your right before turning right down a slope to the canal.

2 Turn left to walk along the tow path with the canal on your right. Enter a dark tunnel **B**, where you will need a torch, as well as the handrail, to guide you. Emerge to continue over an aqueduct **C**, above which is the railway viaduct **D**. Notice a mound **E** below the church away to

your left. Go ahead along the tow path to reach a road (in England).

3 Turn right over the bridge and up the road until you reach a kissing-gate on your right. Turn right along this signposted path, keeping above the canal on your right.

4 Cross the railway with care and continue beside a fence and trees on your right. Switch sides by taking a stile and putting the hedge on your left. Descend along the woodland path which was once part of the Glyn Valley Tramway.

5 Bear right down a lane. Ignore the first turning on your left, pass a dovecote **F** and turn left, before the bridge. When this lane

bends left, just after a telephone box, cross a stile beside a gate on your right. Follow the meadow path with the River Ceiriog on your right.

6 Continue over a stile and through woodland, climbing to a viewpoint overlooking a trout farm on your right. Pass a plaque in memory of Katharine Elizabeth Burrows, 'a lover of nature and this valley'. Cross a stile and bear left, as waymarked.

7 Bear left over a stile beside a blue gate and follow a green lane beneath a magnificent black poplar tree. Go ahead through three gates and continue along a lane. Reach a road and turn right along it for 20 yards (18 metres). Fork

left along a walled track, passing the Old School on your right. Ignore a stile on your left but go ahead over a stile to the right of a gate at the end of the track.

8 Go ahead and pass a footpath signpost on your left. After 10 yards (9 metres) bear left through a broad gap in the hedge. Pass beneath a wooden pole carrying electric cables, continue through a gap in the next hedge, then cross a narrow field to a stile. Cross it and bear left across a track to take a gate in the hedge opposite. Go uphill across the corner of a field to go over wooden bars in the top hedge. Go straight ahead uphill to a gate and follow a rough grassy track above woodland on your right. Go ahead over a stile with a hedge on your left towards a white cottage.

9 Turn right to walk downhill with Offa's Dyke **G** on your left. Veer right to a stile beside a gate to take a hedged path towards the castle on the hill ahead. Go left at a path junction to descend to a road. Cross it — if you wish to divert to the lime kilns **H** they are on your right — and bear left down to the bridge over the River Ceiriog **J** and the B4500.

10 Veer left up a 'No Through Road' waymarked with the Offa's Dyke Path

acorn symbol. Pass a forest track on your right, bear right at a fork ahead and bear right, as waymarked, after passing a farmyard. Climb to a signpost and turn right over a stile. Go ahead to reach a lodge at Tyn-y-groes, where the road bends.

11 Turn right to cross a stile and follow the courtesy path, open from Easter to the end of September, which is waymarked with white-topped posts. Follow a track with a wall on your right. A lake **K** can be seen across the field on your

left. Reach Home Farm and fork left at a letterbox to follow the drive and pass Chirk Castle **L** on your right. Go through the car park and turn right up to the castle.

12 Return to the car park but turn right over a stile to take a signposted path. Pass a haha **M** on your right. Cross the parkland, going through a gate and walking with a fence on your right. Bear right over a stile to cross a field diagonally along a waymarked path. Continue through a gate in a corner and beside a fence on your

right to reach a road at the cottage Llwyn-y-cil **N**.

13 Bear right across the road to go over a waymarked stile and follow power lines across a field. Enter woodland and bear right to walk above the canal on your left. Cross a stile to a road and go left back to the station. Alternatively, at Llwyn-y-cil, turn right and follow the road to the main entrance to Chirk Castle with its magnificent wrought-iron gates. Follow the road round to the left and continue over the canal and railway to the station.

and the trucks were drawn by horses. Between 1873 and 1888 the eastern terminus was the canal at Chirk Bank. The introduction of steam-hauled services in 1888 led to a new terminus at Chirk Station.

Slate and, later, granite was carried along a track running on the Welsh (north) side of the River Ceiriog west of Pont-faen Bridge. In 1891 passenger trains were introduced; they finally succumbed to rival bus services in 1933. The line closed to all traffic in 1935. At its peak, however, it had four locomotives, 14 passenger coaches, 258

◄Chirk Hatchery was established in 1901 to rear trout and restock the local pools and rivers.

wagons and a staff of 32. If you want to see a single surviving coach, go to the Tal-y-llyn Railway in Gwynedd.

The canal is a wildlife reserve. The section of the walk that follows the viaduct goes through the reserve where there are dragonflies, butterflies, water skaters and water boatmen. In the water are roach, perch, bream, rudd, pike, tench and carp, with coot and moorhen above. The valley is rich in birdlife, including wagtails, dippers, skylarks, meadow pipits, green woodpeckers, hedge sparrows, blackbirds, thrushes, crows and magpies. There are blackberries, foxgloves, rosebay willow herbs and yellow pimpernel. Primroses adorn the woodland in spring, when there is the smell of wild garlic.

THE DARK TUNNEL

The dark tunnel **B** is 459 yards (414 metres) long and shows the power of the owner of Chirk Castle, for it was built to preserve his view. Since 1963 it has been called the Llangollen Canal, but was originally the Ellesmere Canal, planned in

1791 to link the River Severn with the Rivers Dee and Mersey. It was never completed because of financial problems, but it did link with the Chester Canal in 1805. The canal passed into the hands of the London and North Western Railway, which

▶Offa's Dyke, still a natural border between England and Wales, runs through the gardens of this cottage.

A Marcher Bastion

The 18th-century landscaped park of Chirk Castle contains a lake that drowns part of Offa's Dyke. Chirk Castle was completed in 1310. It was built by the Marcher Lord Roger Mortimer to consolidate Edward I's conquest of Wales in 1282. Instead of providing the English crown with security in Wales, though, it provided a long list of traitors. At least five of its owners had been executed for treason before the estate was sold to Thomas Myddleton in 1595. His descendants are still here, although the castle was acquired by the National Trust in 1978.

The castle was badly damaged by Parliamentary artillery during the Civil War. Its 15-foot (4.5-metre) thick walls are aligned on the cardinal points of the compass and its four corner towers are 47 feet (14 metres) in diameter. Its appearance has changed little, with a courtyard enclosed by high sandstone walls and massive drum towers. It has been restored and converted into a stately home with elegant plasterwork distinguishing the interior. The parkland has a haha built in a ditch to keep in livestock without causing an obstruction to the view from the castle. As you leave the grounds, notice the timber-framed cottage. Its end wall probably dates from the 15th century, while the timbers may have been recycled from galleons.

Chirk Castle was completed in 1301 and has many superb rooms and landscaped gardens. The wrought-iron gates (inset) date back to 1719.

▲ Beautiful views of the River Ceiriog in its lush green setting can be had from the track between stages 10 and 11.

ran it in competition with the trains of the Great Western Railway.

Thomas Telford and William Jessop built the aqueduct ● at Chirk. Its construction took from 1796 to 1801 and it stands 70 feet (21 metres) above the River Ceiriog. It is 696 feet (209 metres) long and 11 feet (3.5 metres) wide, within which width is the iron trough containing the canal. There are 10 arches, each with a span of 40 feet (12 metres). Overlooking it is the railway viaduct ●. This fine example of Victorian architecture was built in 1848 for the Great Western Railway by Henry Robertson, who was notorious for surveying the land by night to avoid hostile landowners. It has 10 arches, each with a span of 45 feet (13.5 metres) and housemartins love to nest on it. At 286 yards (257

metres) in length, it stands 100 feet (30 metres) above the valley floor.

The aqueduct is a fine vantage point. Notice the church away to your left. This is now dedicated to St Mary. Chirk may be a corruption of church or kirk, although the Welsh name is 'Y Waun', meaning 'The Moor'. The village guarded the River Ceiriog, so the Normans built a motte and bailey just below the church in the early 12th century. The remaining mound ● marks the site of the original Castell y Waun.

Following the Maelor Way, a 24-mile- (38.6-km-) long route linking the Offa's Dyke Path west of Chirk with Cheshire's Sandstone Trail,

near Whitechurch, notice the remains of a dovecote ●. There are small square holes in the end wall of a barn, dated 1778. Eventually you will reach the Offa's Dyke Path at a well-preserved part of the dyke ●. This was erected by King Offa of Mercia in the late 8th century. It still forms the national border here, although you do not return to Wales until you descend to the bridge over the River Ceiriog. Dally in England by diverting about 150 yards (135 metres) eastwards along the road to see the limekilns ● at Bronygarth. These processed lime from the quarries for use as a field dressing.

The gap in Offa's Dyke formed by the River Ceiriog ● is known as the Pass of the Graves (Ardwyr Beddau). The Battle of Crogen was fought here in 1165, when Henry II invaded Wales with an army of mercenaries, including some from Anjou. Heavily defeated by the valiant Welsh, Henry retaliated by blinding and castrating hostages.

▶ Trees of Chirk Castle parkland silhouetted against the early morning light suggest a tranquil walk.

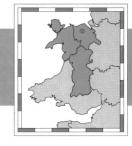

The impressive remains of Denbigh Castle stand on a hill overlooking the town. Much of the town walls also remain. Look for the azure damselfly (inset below) along the riverside.

Robert Dudley, Earl of Leicester, was one of Queen Elizabeth I's favourites and was Lord of Denbigh from 1563 until his death in 1588. The foundation stone was laid in 1578 and this was to be the first great new church to be built in Protestant Britain (preceding the cathedral at Londonderry by 30 years).

The building was never finished, but tradition has it that Leicester meant it to replace the cathedral church of nearby St Asaph. Its first vicar was William Morgan, renowned for translating the Bible into Welsh.

The tower below the castle did not belong to Leicester's church but to the 13th-century garrison and

FACT FILE

- Denbigh, Clwyd
- Pathfinder 772 (SJ 06/16), grid reference SJ 052661

  miles 0 1 2 3 4 5 6 7 8 9 10 miles
  kms 0 1 2 3 4 5 6 7 8 9 10 11 12 13 14 15 kms

- Allow 3 hours
- A few moderate climbs. The meadows may be muddy so take waterproof shoes
- P Car parks are signposted in Denbigh (off Factory Ward or near the castle entrance)
- T Denbigh is served by buses nos 49 and 50 from Abergele, no 51 from Rhyl and Corwen and no 52 between Rhyl and Mold. The nearest British Rail station is at Rhyl
- In Denbigh
- WC In Denbigh
- Denbigh Castle open daily May-Sept from 10am-5pm; Oct-April from 9.30am-4pm

Through woodland and meadow around a beautiful Welsh castle

Denbigh is a fine example of a medieval walled town. Its castle stands on a hilltop with the Clwydian Range as its backdrop. According to legend, Denbigh's name originated in the Middle Ages when one Sion Bodiau (John of the thumbs, of which he had two on each hand) killed a dragon near the castle. 'Dim bych!' shouted the people, meaning 'no more dragons'. This was corrupted to Dinbych. The less romantic may prefer to point out that Dinbych means 'small fortified place'.

The walk begins in the town at the County Hall. As you turn the corner along Bull Lane, notice the North Eastern Tower **A**. The town wall has a break in it, where you bear left to pass the site of Lord Leicester's church **B** on your left.

THE WALK

DENBIGH

The walk begins at the old County Hall at the head of Denbigh's High Street.

1 Facing the County Hall, go right into Hall Square and turn right up Bull Lane. Pass a signposted path going left at a corner below the town wall's North Eastern Tower **A**. Go right with the lane and bear left to pass the site of Leicester's church **B** and reach Hilary's Tower. Go ahead to Denbigh Castle **C**.

2 Continue below the castle which is on your left along a lane which descends to a road. Go left until you reach a rough lane on your left, just before Trefeirian Social Club.

3 Taking the rough lane on your left, go straight ahead along a signposted path when the lane forks left after 50 yards (45 metres). The wall on your left gives way to woodland as you descend to a kissing gate in the hedge on your right. Turn right through it and follow the hedge on your right to a signpost in next corner. Bear left down following field to another signpost.

4 Turn right to walk with a hedge on your left.

Continue over a slate slab footbridge and through a kissing gate. Cross a farm track in the next corner through the gate ahead and continue beside a hedge on your right. Maintain your direction through a gate and descend to a signpost.

5 Turn right along the narrow, hedged path, down to a road. Turn right uphill.

6 Turn left through a gate to follow the signposted path past the psychiatric hospital **D** which is behind the wall on your right. Ignore a lane which goes right and descend past a sports ground on your left. Pass a house on your right, ignore a stile beside a gate ahead and veer right beside a fence on your left. Continue above a river on your left and emerge from woodland to cross a meadow.

7 Cross a stile in the hedge on your right and go right along a road for 100 yards (90 metres). Turn sharply left along a signposted path. After a woodland walk above the river (Afon Ystrad) on your left, emerge into a meadow. The ruined cottage **E** used by Dr Samuel Johnson is immediately on your right, hidden by trees. Continue

across the meadow, veering away from the river to a stile beside a gate in the far corner.

8 Go over the stile to re-enter woodland. You will return here, but first take the woodland path ahead, then bear left down a meadow. A monument **F** to Dr Johnson can be seen under trees near the river. Retrace your steps through the woodland but do not re-enter the meadow with the cottage. Go left before reaching it and uphill to a stile in the woodland fence.

9 Continue uphill to a track and go right along it. Cross a stile beside a gate and go left with the track to the top corner of the next field. Go ahead across another field and over the stile by the gate. Then bear right to follow a wall on your right.

10 Cross the drive of Gwaynynog **G** and follow the track across the field ahead. Keep left with the

track in the following field, cross a stile beside a gate in its corner and continue beside a hedge on your left. Take a gate in the next corner and walk with the hedge still on your left down to a stile. This leads to a track which takes you past Galch Hill **H**.

11 Turn left along a signposted path and cross the field diagonally (aiming for the tall trees just to the right of the castle beyond). Turn left to follow a hedge on your right. Go ahead over a stile to bear right along an enclosed path behind houses and gardens.

12 Go left along Llewelyn's Estate road. Cross a main road and turn right for 20 yards (18 metres). Turn left through a kissing-gate along a signposted path which continues as Glas Meadow Lane to Smithfield Road. Turn right, pass The Hand Inn **J** on your left and return to the High Street.

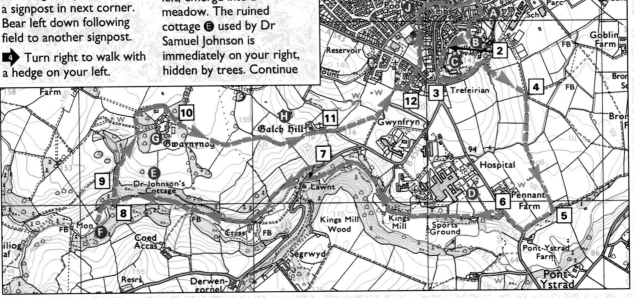

town chapel of St Hilary's, the church it was meant to replace.

Between St Hilary's Tower and the main entrance of Denbigh Castle stood the birthplace of one of the most interesting figures of the Victorian period. Henry Morton Stanley, the explorer and journalist, was born here in 1841 as John Rowlands, the illegitimate son of Elizabeth Parry and John Rowlands.

He suffered a dreadfully harsh childhood, spending eight years in St Asaph workhouse. Fortunately, he managed to get an education there and he later worked briefly as a teacher.

HOTSPUR'S CASTLE

In 1859 he crossed the Atlantic to New Orleans as a cabin boy. There he met Henry Morton Stanley, the benefactor whose name he was to adopt. It was on 10th November 1871 that he walked into the history books with the famous words 'Dr Livingstone, I presume?'

The walk passes below Denbigh

against Henry IV. In 1468, Jasper Tudor burned down the town during the Wars of the Roses while, in 1646, the defending Royalists were besieged there for six months before surrendering to the Parliamentarians. The castle is now in the care of CADW and is open to the public. The walk passes the 19th-century lunatic

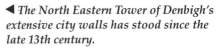
◀ The North Eastern Tower of Denbigh's extensive city walls has stood since the late 13th century.

Nature Walk

The body and wings of the mature male BLACK REDSTART are sooty black, except for white patches on the wings and grey underparts. The female is grey-brown above and below. Both have a reddish-brown tail. The Old English for tail is 'steort', hence the name redstart.

Castle ● which stands in ruins today but still gives the impression of might. There was probably a native Welsh fort on this site before Edward I of England conquered Wales and gave the newly created lordship of Denbigh to Henry de Lacy, Earl of Lincoln. The castle was practically complete by the time of the Earl's death in 1311.

Henry Percy (Shakespeare's Hotspur) held the castle in 1403 and joined forces with Owain Glyndwr

▲ Leicester's Folly, the ruins of an unfinished cathedral, was started in the 16th century by the Earl of Leicester.

▶ Sun-dappled woodlands on the banks of Afon Ystrad.

asylum **D**, still in use as a psychiatric hospital.

Dr Samuel Johnson also came this way. He is said to have stayed in the ruined cottage **E**. The monument **F** was erected by the local clergyman, Mr Myddelton, during Dr Johnson's lifetime, to his great annoyance. On one side is carved:

'This spot was often dignified by the Presence of Samuel Johnson LLD whose moral writings exactly con-

▶ *Sweeping views over meadows and woodland seen while climbing the slope from the Afon Ystrad.*

Back in the town, the Hand Inn **J** took its name from the legend of a race being held to settle a dispute about an inheritance. A supporter of the runner lying second cut off the first man's hand to prevent it making the winning touch. It became the Myddelton coat of arms.

▲ *Dr Samuel Johnson, a famous visitor to Denbigh, is commemorated by this monument near the Afon Ystrad.*

formable to the Precepts of Christianity, give ardour to Virtue and Confidence to Truth'.

HAND ON ARMS

Gwaynynog **G** was also visited by Dr Johnson who described it as 'a gentleman's house, below the second rate, perhaps below the third, built of stone roughly cut. The rooms were low, and the passage above the stairs gloomy, but the furniture was good. The table was well supplied, except that the fruit was bad. It was truly the dinner of a country gentleman.' Notice the ha-ha (ditch) around the house.

Further along the route is the black and white Tudor farmhouse of Galch Hill **H**, the birthplace of Sir Thomas Myddelton who bought Chirk Castle in 1595 and became Lord Mayor of London in 1613.

The Great Lexicographer

Dr Samuel Johnson travelled to Denbigh with his companion Mrs Thrale in 1774, and they stayed with Mr Myddelton in a cottage in the grounds of Gwaynynog house. Johnson visited Gwaynynog wood which he found 'diversified and romantic' and generally seemed to enjoy his stay. He was not as disparaging of the Welsh as of the Scots, though he did say:

'Let us jump over the Afon Ystrad [the local river] directly, and show them how an Englishman should treat a Welsh river'.

Dr Johnson was renowned as a great wit, as much as for compiling the first dictionary in 1751. This gave the meanings of some 50,000 words, one of which was lexicographer. Johnson defined this as a 'writer of dictionaries: a harmless drudge that busies himself in tracing the original and detailing the significance of words'.

He left behind him many famous anecdotes. One was a reference to his dictionary being completed before a similar French effort. He declared:

'Why, what would you expect, dear Sir, from fellows that eat frogs?'

Johnson was born in Lichfield and was not particularly wealthy. In fact, he was forced by poverty to give up his degree course at Oxford University. He was a prodigious worker, producing virtually single-handedly what would now require an army of experts and editors — and all of this in spite of his being blind in one eye! He also suffered from scrofula (a glandular disease, also known as the king's evil) and was 'touched' by Queen Anne to cure it.

Dr Johnson is said to have stayed in a cottage, now ruined, in the grounds of Gwaynynog house when he visited Denbigh in the summer of 1774. This painting by Dante Gabriel Rossetti in the Tate Gallery shows Johnson, second from left, and his biographer Boswell dining with two companions.

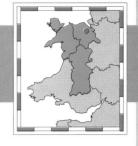
A walk to a mysterious hillfort in the Clwydian Range

A bare, rounded hill with a small cone rising to 1,494 feet (455 metres) is the focal point of this walk. It provides magnificent views, but it is harder to define the mystery of its legends and its name.

Llwybr Clawdd Offa (Offa's Dyke Path) Ⓐ is followed for the first mile of this walk. This 177-mile (285-km) route became Britain's fourth official Long Distance Path (now called a National Trail) in 1971. Although named after the 8th-century dyke, this section follows the scenic hills of the Clwydian Range rather than the remnants of either Offa's Dyke or the earlier Wat's Dyke which lie to the east of it.

TO THE SUMMIT

Impressive triple lines of defence form the hillfort on the summit of Moel Arthur Ⓑ. This is just one of several hillforts strung along the Clwydian Range. These forts were used for defence during the Bronze Age — axe heads from this period have been found here. Coarse Roman pottery has also been

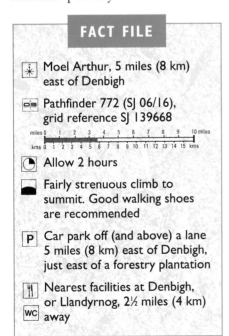

FACT FILE

- Moel Arthur, 5 miles (8 km) east of Denbigh

- Pathfinder 772 (SJ 06/16), grid reference SJ 139668

  miles 0 1 2 3 4 5 6 7 8 9 10 miles
  kms 0 1 2 3 4 5 6 7 8 9 10 11 12 13 14 15 kms

- Allow 2 hours

- Fairly strenuous climb to summit. Good walking shoes are recommended

- P Car park off (and above) a lane 5 miles (8 km) east of Denbigh, just east of a forestry plantation

- Nearest facilities at Denbigh, or Llandyrnog, 2½ miles (4 km) WC away

▲The bare, rounded cone of Moel Arthur in the Clwydian Hills is steeped in history. Often found on heathland, the emperor moth (left) displays its prominent eyespots. Two of the hillfort's lines of defence (below), now overgrown with heather.

unearthed, so it is possible that the site was inhabited in the 6th century, when the legendary King Arthur commanded the British forces.

Whether Arthur is involved with a treasure chest reputedly buried near the summit is not clear. Perhaps it is connected with Boudicca, the English warrior-queen, who may have been buried here. As legend has it, a supernatural light sometimes shows where the chest is buried, while a grey lady is also said to appear. Once she gave peas to a

THE WALK

MOEL ARTHUR

The walk begins from an official country park car park at the end of a forestry plantation on your left, as you take a minor road east from Denbigh.

1 ▶ Go down to the road from the car park and turn right along it for 150 yards (135 metres)

2 ▶ Turn left over a stile to follow the signposted Offa's Dyke Path **A**. (This is a newly waymarked path, which is not shown on old editions of the Pathfinder map.) The path veers left uphill. Acorn symbols and yellow arrows guide you through scrubland and a steep climb leads to a stile. Go ahead over this stile and the next one, and then take the well-defined path leading through the heather to meet a fence on your left.

3 ▶ When you are level with a gate and a waymark post on your left, turn right up a path to the summit of Moel Arthur **B**. Retrace your steps and resume your former direction. Leave the fence on your left when a waymark post shows you to bear right down to a road. On the way, notice the steep slope on your right **C**.

4 ▶ Go right along the road, crossing a cattle grid. Leave the Offa's Dyke Path as it heads south to Chepstow, 153 miles (246 km) away. Follow the road around a bend on your right.

5 ▶ Turn right through a gate and follow a track running beside a fence on your left. Continue through a gate and pass a pond on your right, below the remains of an old farmhouse.

6 ▶ Take a gate ahead and fork right. Follow this track as it swings right to a stile beside a gate. Cross this to go down to a farm access lane.

7 ▶ Cross the lane to walk with a fence on your right and above a farm on your left. Turn right through a gate when you are below the farm. Follow a hedge on your right until you are half-way down the field, then descend diagonally left to take a gate in the bottom hedge to reach a road.

8 ▶ Go left to follow the road around a bend on your right, then turn right up a forest track.

9 ▶ Bear right at a fork to take the grassy track uphill through the plantation **D**. Go ahead across the gravel track to climb back to the car park.

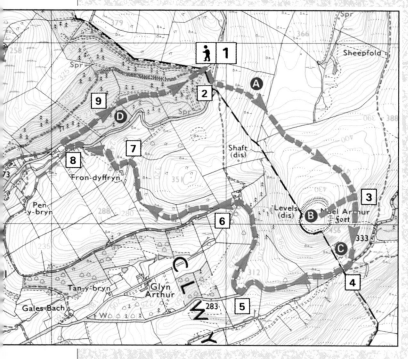

man and ordered him home, where he found they had changed into pieces of gold!

On a fine day, there are views over Denbigh in the valley to the west, or even of Blackpool Tower beyond Liverpool (whose Anglican cathedral can be distinguished) to the north-east.

PURPLE HEATHER

As you descend, notice the steep slope on your right **C**. This used to be a notorious ascent for backpackers bound for Prestatyn, before the trail was diverted. Here you can enjoy the purple heather of the hill and a fine display of gorse, whose prickly yellow-flowered shrubs occupy the edges of fields. Llangwyfan forestry plantation **D** is stocked with foreign conifers. Above you, to the north, is Penycloddian, the largest hillfort in the Clwydian Range.

▶ *The view from the stile in Stage 6 of the walk, which brings you to the farm access lane. Llangwyfan forestry plantation can be seen in the background. It consists largely of coniferous trees for timber production. Such plantations have changed the appearance of Britain's uplands.*

DYSERTH FALLS

▲*Offa's Dyke Path leaves the dyke and runs along the Clwydian Hills, providing views of the Irish Sea beyond Prestatyn. Lady's bedstraw (left) grows in the grassland around here. Water tumbles through a rocky cleft at Dyserth Falls (right) into a quiet pool.*

From a waterfall with healing powers to Offa's Dyke Path

U p in this north-eastern corner of Wales, the Clwydian range of hills terminates in a limestone escarpment overlooking the coastal resorts of Rhyl and Prestatyn. Over the centuries, this escarpment has been an easy site to defend in troubled times and a useful source of lime and lead. Now, it is a tourist attraction with fine views.

Dyserth Falls Ⓐ were once a centre for pilgrimages, as the waters were reputed to have healing qualities. Later, the falls provided power for the flour mill that stood behind the present Waterfalls Shop. The shop itself was originally the stables of Y Llew Coch (the Red Lion pub). Until the advent of the railway in the 19th century, Dyserth was accessible only by coach or on horseback.

QUARRIED AWAY

Further on, a steep craggy hill on the right was originally the site of an Iron Age hill-fort, but the remains of this were largely destroyed by quarrying in the mid-19th century. Stone and lime were excavated at Ochr-y-foel and this was a major reason for the opening of the railway line from Prestatyn in 1869. As the quarries became more important, the railway was extended to meet the workings.

From the disused railway bridge there are views of Dyserth Station Ⓑ on the left and the extended railway siding bearing right towards the

FACT FILE

- ✳ Dyserth, 2 miles (3.2km) south of Prestatyn

- ⌖ Pathfinders 737 (SJ 08/18) and 755 (SJ 07/17), grid reference SJ 056793

  miles 0 1 2 3 4 5 6 7 8 9 10 miles
  kms 0 1 2 3 4 5 6 7 8 9 10 11 12 13 14 15 kms

- ◔ Allow 2½ hours

- ⌒ Undulating countryside. Boots advisable in wet weather

- Ⓟ Free car park at Dyserth Falls

- 🍴 Red Lion pub and a café at Dyserth Falls

- wc At the car park

THE WALK

DYSERTH FALLS – GRAIG FAWR

The starting point is the Dyserth Falls car park.

1 The footpath to Dyserth Falls **A** starts behind the Waterfalls Shop. Follow it past the falls and up steps between two stone walls. At the top, bear right by a bench and continue up to an open area with views of Rhyl and the coastal plain. A path leads from the back of this area, through some trees, down to a wider path. Follow this and cross a stile. Turn right and then bear left up to a field. Carry straight on across the field until a red-roofed cottage is visible, then aim for a stile to the left of it.

2 Cross the stile and follow the path through woods to a road. Cross the road to a flight of iron steps leading to a path across a field. Soon, you reach a disused railway bridge overlooking the site of Dyserth Station **B**. Climb over a stile and cross a field, to a stile and ditch leading to a track. Turn sharp left and follow the track past a quarry to a gate. Ignore the gate and follow the fence on the right, keeping it on your left. Cross two more stiles to come to a road.

3 Turn left and follow the road to a crossroads. By a car park is the entrance to the conservation area surrounding Graig Fawr **C**. Walk to the summit of this hill for some spectacular views over Rhyl, Prestatyn and the coastal plain. Return to the road.

4 Turn left and follow the road. Ignore a waymarked path to the left. At a T-junction, turn left and then immediately right. This is Offa's Dyke Path **D**, marked by acorn signs. Continue following the acorn markers along the clifftop path, climbing steadily, to a junction.

5 Take the steep downhill path that forks left through scrub and trees to the bottom of the escarpment. Turn right onto a road for a short distance. Opposite a house named 'Mandalay' descend some brick steps and continue across a golf course. Just before the clubhouse is a disused railway track bed **E**.

6 Turn left along the track bed and follow it for nearly 1½ miles (2.4km), passing under the rocky outcrops of Graig Fawr and crossing over three disused railway bridges. At a stone road-bridge over the track bed, turn left just past it, up to the road. Cross the bridge and walk along the lane, ignoring a right turn. Continue to the iron steps you climbed earlier. Turn right at the steps and retrace your route.

quarry. A few fields further on is a fine view of the site of Dyserth Castle, built by Henry III in 1241.

The short climb to the summit of Graig Fawr **C** is well worth it for the spectacular views towards Rhyl and Prestatyn. Underneath this hill, lead mines used to provide work for the Victorian inhabitants of Meliden.

Now, the site is owned by the National Trust, and is a designated conservation area for many species of limestone-loving flowers, such as wild thyme, kidney vetch, bird's foot trefoil and common rock-rose.

The next section of the walk includes part of the Offa's Dyke Path **D**. The dyke itself actually ran eastwards of here. Built by Offa, an 8th-century Mercian king, as a boundary to his kingdom, this earth wall is nearly 150 miles (240km) long and runs from the Irish Sea southwards to the Bristol Channel.

DAY-TRIPPERS

At the foot of the escarpment, the old railway track bed **E**, passes the Graig Fawr Quarry and the Talaroch Lead Mine. Although the railway was originally built for freight, it opened for passenger traffic in 1905. At the time, Prestatyn was fast developing as a seaside resort, and rail trips to see the falls were a popular attraction for tourists.

◀ *The metalled track bed runs past a rocky outcrop of Graig Fawr. The hill was once mined extensively for lead.*

CLWYD

boundaries in the 18th century. The block-headed behaviour of the parties involved was satirized in the sign of the inn across the road from the park entrance. It depicts two figures back to back, clearly not on speaking terms. This sign is attributed to Richard Wilson, an early landscape painter, who lived locally.

The River Alyn runs along a glaciated valley through the heart of the country park, and its course is followed for about the first two miles (3.2km) of the walk.

This is limestone country, covered

FACT FILE

✻ Loggerheads Country Park, 10½ miles (16.8km) north-west of Wrexham

🗺 Pathfinder 772 (SJ 06/16), grid reference SJ 198626

miles 0   1   2   3   4   5   6   7   8   9   10 miles
kms 0 1 2 3 4 5 6 7 8 9 10 11 12 13 14 15 kms

◔ Allow 4½ hours

▬ A long, steady climb; it is more than 1,300 feet (400m) from the start to the summit of Moel Fammau. Boots are advisable

Ⓟ At the start

🍴 We Three Loggerheads pub and a café at the start

WC At the start

Ⓘ Information Centre on the nature trail and the industrial trail at the start

Through limestone country to a spectacular viewpoint

▲ *The limestone escarpment forms an imposing backdrop to the woodlands of Loggerheads Country Park. A common garden plant, the rose of Sharon (inset) grows wild here, flowering in summer.*

This walk begins in Loggerheads Country Park, a long established beauty spot that is popular with both those seeking rural peace and those whose interest is industrial archaeology.

Loggerheads, in principle if not in name, was a pioneer of the concept of a country park. Industry had virtually ceased here by the turn of the century, and in 1926 the Crosville Motor Bus Company bought the land to develop as a tourist venue for their bus trips. A tea house, bandstand, boating lakes and kiosks

were installed and gardens were laid out in the style of an urban park. It was extremely popular in the 1930s, when the hourly bus service brought the crowds from nearby towns. The land was bought by Clwyd in 1974 and turned into a country park proper, with a fine nature trail and an industrial trail.

The area got its unusual name from an acrimonious dispute over

▶ *Showing every sign of a quarrel, these figures symbolize the boundary dispute that gave the area its unusual name.*

THE WALK

LOGGERHEADS – MOEL FAMMAU

The walk starts from the Information Centre at Loggerheads Country Park, on the A494 3 miles (4.8km) west of Mold.

1 ▶ Follow the Industrial Trail signs by the Information Centre buildings to reach Pentre Mill **A**. Continue to follow the Industrial Trail as it goes across the River Alyn. Climb some steps to where the Industrial and Nature Trails converge.

2 ▶ Follow the trails to the left. At Nature Trail Post 8 the river begins to disappear down swallow holes **B**. Continue along this path to a kissing-gate. The Nature Trail goes right but you follow the Leete Walk through the gate and past a boarding kennels to join a stony lane. This soon goes through a gate to meet a tarmac lane, where you branch left on a marked path into some woods. Continue to follow the leat **C**, which becomes more pronounced, then disappears into a tunnel where another path crosses it. Continue along the level to rejoin the leat. After a while the drop to the river becomes a precipice and soon a footbridge crosses a deep fissure in the rock.

3 ▶ At a crossroads of paths, the way ahead is often closed because of falling rocks. If it is open, go along it to where it meets a road and turn left. If it is closed, turn right uphill and cross a stile. A grassy path through gorse leads to a field. Cross this to some sheep pens. Turn left along a lane and continue to a T-junction. Turn left. The road bears right, then swings left down a hill, where you meet the other end of the closed section of path.

4 ▶ Follow the road across a narrow bridge, then up into some woods. When it bends sharp right, take a clear path to the left signposted 'Pentre'. This skirts a succession of fields and enters some woods. At a junction with a bridleway (blue arrow), turn right past a small reservoir on your left, then left, downhill, on a minor road.

5 ▶ At a road junction, turn right. Go past Pentre Farm. The road doubles back to the right, but you continue ahead by following a stony track.

6 ▶ Turn left down a

▲ *A reminder of the days when this woodland haven was used for lead mining, an activity that ceased in 1870.*

with woodland. Ash, alder, hazel and sycamore favour the riverside area, with ferns, lichens and woodland flowers growing beneath the tree canopy. Treecreepers, jays and nuthatches live in the woods, while grey wagtails, dippers and grey herons haunt the river.

NESTING BIRDS

On the steep slopes of the valley sides, oak, beech and silver birch mingle with conifers, while shrubs and undergrowth provide a healthy environment for a wide variety of birdlife. More than 50 bird species nest in the country park.

This woodland paradise was once an industrial environment. Mills are found all along the valley. Pentre Mill **Ⓐ**, at the start of the walk, dates from the 1820s, though there was probably an earlier building on the site. Initially it produced flour and animal feed for local consumption, though a saw pit was added when it was bought by a carpenter. Flour milling ceased in 1920, when the mill-wheel was attached to a dynamo to provide electricity for nearby dwellings.

DISAPPEARING RIVER

Shortly after crossing the River Alyn (Nature Trail Post 8) you come to a place where it seasonally dries up; the flow decreases steadily as you go. The water disappears into swallow holes **Ⓑ**, natural fissures in

◀ *Pentre Mill, which used to produce flour and animal feed, is just one of the many mills in the area that took its water supply from the River Alyn (right) during the 19th century.*

the limestone that have been enlarged by erosion, and runs underground through caves.

Further on, along the section known as the Leete Walk, you can see great caves and fissures in the rock. Some of these features, which may have been natural originally, have been exploited by man, because the area was a centre for lead mining up to the 1870s.

Mining in this type of rock presented some problems, as water seeped down through the cracks to flood the deeper levels. One answer was to use pumps powered by

marked path at the entrance to Tyddyn-y-foel farm and then right over a stone stile. Continue across two fields, keeping a hedge on your left, and cross a lane to a bridleway opposite. Cross a stile by a gate and go straight on up a grassy path past a reservoir on your left. Continue along this path up the valley to climb steeply out of the end, where it crosses another bridleway before a

conifer forest.

7 Go straight on up the marked footpath to the summit of Moel Fammau **Ⓓ** and the Jubilee Tower. Retrace your steps to the bridleway by the conifer forest, and turn right. Go through a gate and follow a stone wall along the edge of the forest to its corner. Cross the ruined wall and a fence to a field. The bridleway skirts Ffrith Mountain to the left, but

you go right around this rounded hill, just above the tree line. Follow a well-worn path from a gate and stile to a farm track, which goes through a gate into a lane. Follow this to a minor road.

8 Take a partially concealed path opposite this junction (by a Loggerheads roadsign) which leads down, across a field and a lane, to cross the River Alyn. A short

ascent to the right brings you to the Leete Path. Turn right, and go past the kennels to the kissing-gate.

9 Complete the Nature Trail by climbing the steps to the left and following a clear path through the woods and along the top of the escarpment. Just beyond Nature Trail Post 15, turn right and double back down another path to the Information Centre and the start.

◀Work out in which direction you are looking with the aid of this view indicator on the top of Jubilee Tower.

water-wheels. However, the wheels themselves needed a constant supply which the disappearing river could not provide.

The answer was to build the leat ◉ (leete is an idiosyncratic local spelling). The route follows its course until you cross the river at Pont Newydd. This artificial channel took its supply from the river above the swallow holes and carried it downstream to the wheelpits working the pumps. To keep the water level as high as possible, the leat had a lesser gradient than the

▼The nature trail path stretches ahead, just before the waters of the River Alyn disappear into swallow holes.

river, so the path gets higher above the river as you go along it.

At Pont Newydd you leave the valley of the Alyn, first to follow the course of a tributary stream, Nant Gain, then to climb steadily through farmland and over moors to Moel Fammau ◉. At 1,818 feet (554m), this is the highest point of the

Clwydian Range. These hills run from Prestatyn on the north coast to Llandegla, south of here, to link up with the Berwyn Hills.

The land to the east and west is comparatively low-lying, so the views from the summit are extensive. Runcorn Bridge, spanning the River Mersey, and the sprawl of Liverpool are away to the northeast. On the western horizon, it is possible to pick out the distinctive outlines of Cadair Idris and Snowdon. To the north is the coastal resort of Rhyl and, beyond it, Blackpool Tower, the mountains of the Lake District and the Isle of Man are occasionally visible, but only in the clearest of conditions.

The return route allows you to climb the opposite side of the valley, from which there are fine views back to Moel Fammau. You also complete the nature trail before returning to the start.

The Jubilee Tower

The summit of Moel Fammau is crowned by the remains of the Jubilee Tower, on which the four points of the compass are shown.

Today the tower stands some 30 feet (9m) high and covers an area 40 yards (36m) square. The original tower was built in 1810 to mark the 50th year of King George III's reign, and the foundation ceremony was attended by around 3,000 people. The 115-foot (34.5-m) tower was never quite completed, because funds – public contributions raised £1,436 18s 0d – were insufficient.

In 1862, the top was destroyed by a storm. Plans for repair were drawn up for Queen Victoria's Golden Jubilee in 1887 but there was insufficient interest. In 1895 the subject arose again, when an ambitious plan was mooted to route the railway from Ruthin through the hill. An underground station under the summit was proposed, with a lift to carry tourists to the tower. This, too, came to nothing and no more was done until European Conservation Year in 1970, when

Despite ambitious plans, the Jubilee Tower was never finished, although its substantial remains still grace the top of Moel Fammau.

the remains were made safe. Bonfires have been lit on the summit on important occasions, such as Queen Elizabeth's Coronation in 1953 and the investiture of the Prince of Wales in 1969.

IRON AND ERDDIG

FACT FILE

✳ Felin Puleston, 1 mile (1.6km) south-west of Wrexham, on the A5152

⊙ Pathfinder 806 (SJ 24/34), grid reference SJ 323492

miles 0 1 2 3 4 5 6 7 8 9 10 miles
kms 0 1 2 3 4 5 6 7 8 9 10 11 12 13 14 15 kms

◔ Allow 4 hours plus time to visit the buildings

▬ Generally flat walking on mostly good paths. Some short, sharp ascents; woodland and riverside paths may be muddy

P Felin Puleston car park at start

T BR to Wrexham. Regular bus services. For times and other tourist information, Tel. (01978) 292015

🏠 Black Lion, Bersham

🍴 Erddig Hall

WC At start, Bersham Heritage Centre, King's Mill and Erddig Hall

🏛 Bersham Heritage Centre open Easter-Sept, Mon-Fri 10am-5pm, Sat-Sun noon-5pm; Oct-Easter closes 1 hr earlier. Bersham Ironworks open Easter-Sept, Mon-Fri 1-5pm, Sat-Sun noon-5pm, admission charge. King's Mill open Easter-Sept, Tues-Sun, 10am-5pm, admission charge. Erdigg Hall (National Trust) open Apr-Oct, Sat-Wed noon-5pm, admission charge

▲ *The manicured lawns of Erddig Hall, a 17th-century country house, sweep majestically down to the waterside. Lesser celandine (left) can be found in the country park's woodland.*

Relics of the industrial and domestic past along a river valley

The Clywedog Valley offers a walk of contrasts, muted today by the passage of time, but very stark in the 18th century. It is the site of Erddig Hall, a country house built in the 1680s. The estate, which is now a country park, is a picture of rural peace, yet a little way beyond it to the west is Bersham, a village that was at the leading edge of the Industrial Revolution.

This walk is in two parts, centred at Felin Puleston, and follows the new Clywedog Trail for much of its length. Either part can be walked first or separately, though it is best to ensure that the Erddig section is walked when the house is open.

The route to Bersham follows the valley west, calling first at the Heritage Centre Ⓐ, where displays tell the history of the valley's industry. There was an iron furnace here as early as 1670. In 1753, the lease to the works was taken over by Isaac Wilkinson. In 1763, his sons, John and William, took over, and founded the New Bersham Company. All three men had a terrific flair for invention.

PERFECT BORES

In the mid-18th century, there was a big demand for cannons. The Wilkinsons developed a boring machine which enabled cannon barrels to be

▶ *At Bersham Heritage Centre is this reconstruction of a horse gin, which was used for lifting heavy loads.*

THE WALK

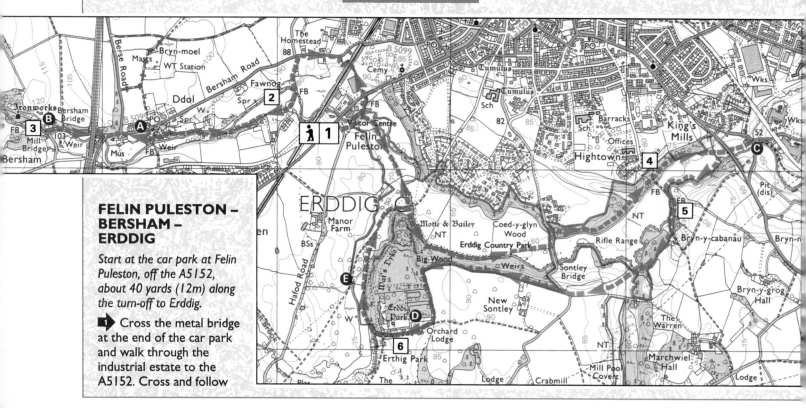

FELIN PULESTON – BERSHAM – ERDDIG

Start at the car park at Felin Puleston, off the A5152, about 40 yards (12m) along the turn-off to Erddig.

1 Cross the metal bridge at the end of the car park and walk through the industrial estate to the A5152. Cross and follow

▲*Wilkinson's Weir was built to supply fast-moving water to Bersham Mill for powering the machinery. King's Mill (right) has recently been renovated.*

cast solid then hollowed out. In 1775, the process was adapted to a much more significant invention, the Boulton and Watt Steam Engine.

Cylinder bores had to be accurate to avoid leakage between them and the pistons. In 1776, James Watt wrote 'Mr Wilkinson has improved the art of boring cylinders so that I promise upon a 72in cylinder being not further from absolute truth than the thickness of a thin sixpence in the worst part.' During the next 20 years, Bersham bored most of the cylinders for Watt's engines, which powered the Industrial Revolution.

Bersham Ironworks expanded and, by the 1790s, employed hundreds of workers and extended for almost half a mile (800m) along the valley. Then, John and William quarrelled and the business drifted into a steady decline.

CANNON FOUNDRY

The Bersham works were closed in 1812. The only part to survive today is at Mill Farm **B**, the furthest point of this section of the walk. The octagonal building here was built as a cannon foundry in about 1775. Bersham Mill, originally a foundry, was converted to a corn mill in 1828. The Mill Farm House was the accounts office.

Other remnants include the weir the Wilkinsons built to provide water to power the machinery, and three cottages opposite the Heritage Centre. These were originally a row of 13, built by the Wilkinsons in 1785 to house their workers. The whole site is being developed as a museum by Clwyd County Council.

the signposted footpath opposite behind a store, through a small wood and up an embankment to the railway. Cross the tracks with care. Go over the stile and down through a small estate to a road. Turn left. In about 300 yards (270m) go left on a waymarked lane, downhill and over a footbridge, then right over a waymarked stile.

2 Follow the left-hand field edge and then the river, to a stile leading to a fenced path. Turn right over the river and left over a cattle grid. Follow the lane over a stile into a village street. Continue along the road. Bear off left by the Black Lion onto a footpath by a brick wall. At the end, turn right up some steps to a children's play area. Cross this to the Heritage Centre **A**. Turn left on the road past the Centre. When this bends left, go ahead under a new bypass, on a road past Wilkinson's Weir, to the old works at Mill Farm **B**.

3 Retrace your steps to the car park at Felin Puleston. Leave it by turning right at the bottom, by a cottage. Follow the path to a gate; cross the stile and continue on a clear track across farmland to another gate. Continue to a stone bridge. Cross and immediately turn right along the river. Continue over a small wooden bridge by a sluice gate and weir to a stile in a stone wall to the left of an iron bridge. Go over the stile to a metalled road. Turn left and follow the wall on the right to a kissing-gate. Go through onto the path in the wood. Eventually this comes to a stile. Cross into the meadow on your right.

4 Continue along the left side of the field, then bear right towards the river and a culvert under the embankment of a new road. A path through the culvert leads to King's Mill **C**. Return through the culvert and follow the river to a wooden footbridge.

5 Cross the bridge and bear right, following the river along an undulating path through woodland. This crosses a new bridge and leads up, over a stile, away from the river into a field. Follow an earth track up the hill to a stile at the far end. Go over this and turn left up the road for 30 paces to a kissing-gate on the right. Go through and follow a clear path to Big Wood. Keep left along the wall of Erddig gardens. Two kissing-gates bring you to the dovecote and the car park for the house **D**.

6 Leave Erddig at the exit for the A483 and turn right at the signpost for the Cup and Saucer **E**. This will take you down past the front of the house and on across a small stone bridge. Turn left just before a second stone bridge — the one crossed on your outward journey — and retrace your steps to return to the car park.

◄ *The formal garden at Erddig displays a distinct low countries' influence, exemplified by this Dutch-gabled roof.*

renovated it as a tourist attraction. There is a working overshot wheel and presentations on the history of the mill and the Clywedog Valley.

The route follows the far side of the river to the woods around Erddig, which are criss-crossed by walks laid out in the 1770s. You approach the house from the rear, with a fine view of the formal gardens through a wrought-iron screen.

In 1716, the Erddig Estate was

The second half of the walk follows the river and passes through woodland in Erddig Country Park to King's Mill **C**, where there has been a mill since at least 1315. The present mill closed in 1940 in disrepair, but Wrexham Maelor Borough Council has now completely

▶ *The 'new' kitchen at Erddig was fitted out with the latest appliances in the 1770s and later, and is a treasure trove of domestic artefacts.*

bought by John Meller. He carried out repairs and the estate passed to his nephew, Simon Yorke, in 1733. He built the current Erddig Hall **D**.

It has been described as 'the most evocative upstairs–downstairs house in Britain'. The Yorke family had an unusually high regard for their servants. John Meller had a portrait painted of a negro coach-boy. This started a remarkable tradition of commissioning portraits of indoor and outdoor staff, which hang alongside those of family members.

This regard for servants is also

Erddig's Formal Garden

The garden at Erddig is, like the house, a rare survival, thanks again to the Yorke family's sense of history outweighing the dictate of fashion. John Meller laid out the garden in its present form between 1718 and 1732 in a style that was then very fashionable. Most contemporary gardens in great houses disappeared under the landscaped vistas that became popular later in the century.

Meller's garden has been fully restored and replanted by the National Trust. The work was greatly helped by an engraving of the gardens made in 1739 by Thomas Badeslade. A list of fruit trees drawn up in 1718 was also invaluable.

The reign of William and Mary (1689-1702) had brought a strong Dutch influence to bear on the country. This was particularly reflected in the gardens of the first part of the 18th century; they tended to be divided into 'rooms' and were used more for producing fruit, vegetables, herbs and flowers for the house than for the recreation of those who lived in it.

The double avenues of pleached limes show where the original garden walls were, before John Meller's reorganization. Trained trees like these were popular during the 17th and 18th centuries. It is thought that the mature limes by the 'canal' were also trained in this way at one time.

Restored by the National Trust after a long period of neglect, Erddig's formal garden is now in immaculate order and is a perfect example of early 18th-century landscaping.

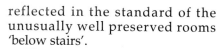

▲*Returning to the start, you pass the Cup and Saucer Waterfall, an intriguing design by William Emes.*

reflected in the standard of the unusually well preserved rooms 'below stairs'.

The last Simon Yorke, who inherited in 1922, faced many problems caused by debts and by Bersham Colliery extending its seams under the house, resulting in structural damage. Time stood still at Erddig. The furniture gathered dust, the roof leaked and the garden became a jungle. Mains water and electricity were never installed, and when Simon died, in 1966, his brother Philip inherited a dangerous building and a garden so overgrown that a carriage was found completely hidden by brambles.

RESTORED SPLENDOUR

Philip, the last of the Yorkes, lived alone in this decaying wilderness until, in 1973, he gave it to the National Trust. He was to see the restoration of the house completed before his death in 1978. It was opened to the public in 1977. Today, Erddig gives a unique insight into the social structure and workings of a traditional country house.

There is one more point of interest on the way back to the start, an unusual feature called the Cup and Saucer **E**. This circular stone basin with a cylindrical waterfall at its centre traps Black Brook, which emerges later through a tunnel. It was created in 1774 by William Emes, who landscaped the park. Incorporated in it is a 19th-century hydraulic ram, which pumps water up to the hall.

A walk around historic sites in a modern moorland landscape

The Llyn Brenig reservoir was built in the 1970s in an area otherwise little changed in 5,000 years. The retreating glaciers at the end of the last Ice Age left drumlins — mounds shaped like upturned boats — littering the landscape. They were formed from the debris left when a glacier passed over an obstruction, such as a rocky outcrop.

The bleak moorland has been put only to seasonal use by man, and the brown hares, grouse, snipe, buzzards and ravens that live here have remained largely undisturbed.

LAKE VIEWS

The addition of the reservoir has softened the bleakness a little and improved the visual appeal of the area. There is a succession of fine views across the lake, as you follow an archaeological trail to visit ancient burial cairns. Some 3,500 years ago, there were substantial settlements further down the valley. Bronze Age people came to these lonely moors to bury their dead.

The first ancient site you pass is the funeral barrow of Boncyn Arian **Ⓐ**, built for a single burial in around 2000BC. The nearby Ring Cairn **Ⓑ** was the focal point for ceremonial cremations for over 400 years. Charcoal was placed in pits against the inner ring of stone. After the cremation, the remains were buried nearby in urns. Two urns recovered here contained the remains of three people, together with a flint knife, pottery ear studs and a small cup.

ROYAL OPENING

The route continues along the banks of Llyn Brenig, which covers 919 acres (370 hectares). Unlike most reservoirs, it does not feed water directly into a piped water supply; it is a regulating reservoir, built to ensure a sufficient supply to the River Dee in times of drought. The water is drawn off at the tower into two shafts, while two further shafts provide access. It was opened by the Prince of Wales in 1976.

Hen Ddinbych (Old Denbigh) **Ⓒ** is a large enclosure surrounded by an earth bank and ditch that measures 65 yards (58m) by 75 yards (67m). There was a stone longhouse

▲ *The prehistoric Ring Cairn stands on the shore of the recently created Llyn Brenig reservoir. Marsh woundwort (right) thrives on the moist soils around the lake.*

FACT FILE

⚹ Llyn Brenig Reservoir, 9 miles (14.6km) west of Ruthin, off the B4501

▣ Pathfinder 787 (SH 94/95), grid reference SH 983574

miles 0 1 2 3 4 5 6 7 8 9 10 miles
kms 0 1 2 3 4 5 6 7 8 9 10 11 12 13 14 15 kms

◗ Allow 1½ hours

▬ Well waymarked walking over rough tracks and open ground. Walking boots are advisable, especially if wet

🄿 At the start

🍴 Nearest refreshments are at Llyn Brenig Information Centre, near the reservoir's dam, Tel. (01490) 420463. Toilets here and at start of walk
ⓦⒸ
ℹ

41

THE WALK

LLYN BRENIG

The walk starts at the car park by the north-eastern corner of Llyn Brenig, just off the B4501.

1 Leave the car park by a stile to head south along an unmetalled road, with the reservoir on your right. Shortly, you come to Boncyn Arian **A** and the Ring Cairn **B**. Continue along the road as it bears left, away from the lake, to Hafoty Siôn Llwyd.

2 Go past the house, crossing the stile by the gate. Follow the track between two fences, then round and up to the right. When the track branches, follow the right fork. Where the track peters out, turn left, uphill. A short, white-topped, waymarker post points you to a circular cairn on a hillock. Bear left towards an artificial-looking plateau, following the white posts to Hen Ddinbych **C**. Follow the direction indicated by the post behind the information plaque, uphill to the Platform Cairn **D**. Continue uphill behind the information plaque, bearing left to walk to another white post. Descend to a gate by a stream.

3 Cross the stream and follow alongside, but below, a broken fence. Where the embankment ends, cross the fence to follow a path. Keep to the left of this field along the top of the slope, which overlooks the outward road. As you pass the first ring cairn, bear right to a white post. Continue uphill, towards the forest, to the Hafotai **E** by a stream. Descend alongside the stream. Cross a wooden bridge to return to the start in the car park.

at one end, with other houses nearby. The remains probably date to the 14th or 15th centuries, but, without excavation, no one can be sure.

The existence of such a large settlement poses something of a mystery. Traditionally, this area was used as summer pasture. The only other buildings on the moors were the small shelters that were used in the summer by the shepherds and cowherds who brought their charges to the high pastures while the home farm concentrated its resources on producing hay for the winter.

▲ *The Platform Cairn, at the walk's halfway point, is the site of a burial ground. The Hafotai, Welsh for 'summer dwellings', on this site (right) were shelters for 16th-century herdsmen.*

Further on is the Platform Cairn **D**, the most impressive ancient site on the walk. It is a circular platform of rocks, some 2 feet (60cm) above ground level, with a diameter of 24 yards (22m). The circle originally had an open centre. An outer ring covered the cremated remains of an adult and child buried, with the bone handle of a dagger, in a pot. A later burial took place in the centre, where a small cairn covered remains surrounded with charcoal. Both events date from after 2000BC.

HAFOD AND HENDRE

The walk ends with a visit to the Hafotai **E**, the remains of a group of stone huts about 450 years old. They were the summer dwellings of shepherds or cowherds, who descended to the 'hendre' (home farm) for the winter. The huts were roofed with rushes and had a central fireplace.

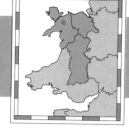
LLYN IDWAL

A lakeside walk in the heart of craggy Snowdonia

This walk gives a real sense of adventuring into a wild mountain region and yet it is both easy and safe. Llyn Idwal lies in a great hollow under the shadow of craggy mountains, ranging from the looming bulk of Tryfan to the spiky ridges of Glyders and the shattered, faintly sinister rocks of the Devil's Kitchen. The Idwal valley was the first National Nature Reserve in Wales (declared in 1954) and is one of the finest. It offers an abundance of plant and bird life on the shores of the lake and up on the crags. The lake itself is shallow, and in its sparkling pure waters you can see minnow and trout.

A RING OF MOUNTAINS

The mountains round the lake change in character along the route. The Idwal slabs **Ⓐ** are hard, smooth rocks of rhyolite (a type of lava), devoid of alpine plants. Their gentle slopes offer good toe- and hand-holds to would-be mountaineers and have become a popular nursery for climbers.

The dramatic Twll Du or Devil's Kitchen **Ⓑ** is a deep, dark chasm slicing into the crags at the south-

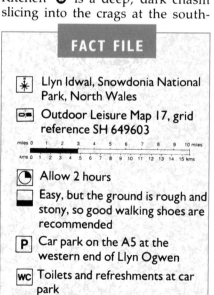

▲ *Cwm Idwal, or the Idwal Valley, was formed by a glacier 10,000 years ago.*
(inset) The Snowdon lily flowers in June.
▶ *Rhaeadr Ogwen, the falls which have to be crossed at the start of the walk.*

west corner of the lake. The down-folded volcanic rock either side of it is evidence of a former mountain range and its ledges are home to a wide variety of mountain plants, including the rare Snowdon lily.

The best view of the ring of mountains is on the west side of the lake **Ⓒ**. Straight across the lake is the massive bulk of Tryfan (3,010 feet/917 metres), which can only be reached by rough scrambling. Following the ridge south you can see Glyder Fach (3,262 feet/994 metres) and then Glyder Fawr (3,279 feet/999 metres) rising high above the

THE WALK

THE IDWAL VALLEY

The walk begins at the car park beside the youth hostel on the A5 at the western end of Llyn Ogwen. The start is clearly marked by a large notice board close to the road.

▶ Cross the footbridge over the mountain stream which rushes between boulders in a torrent of water known as Rhaeadr Ogwen or the Ogwen Falls. Beyond here the stony path is clearly defined, and after a walk of about ½ mile (800 metres), you reach the lake, Llyn Idwal.

▶ The route is one circuit round the lake, most easily followed by walking in a clockwise direction. At the start the path is easily seen, leading to the high, seemingly smooth sloped crags known as the Idwal slabs Ⓐ.

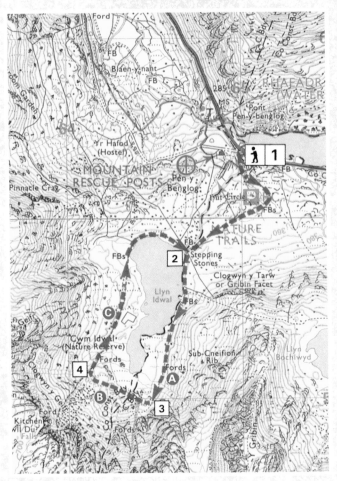

▶ At the foot of the Idwal slabs, turn right on to the narrow rough path leading towards the head of the lake. This brings you to an area of rough, level grassland. Here there is no well-marked path but the area can easily be crossed by keeping just below the rock-strewn steeper slopes below the Devil's Kitchen Ⓑ. Do not attempt to explore the Devil's Kitchen itself unless you are an experienced mountain climber, as it can be very dangerous. The path on the opposite side of the lake can clearly be seen.

▶ When you reach the path on the other side of the lake, turn right to complete the circuit of the lake. You have the best view of the mountains from Ⓒ. At **2** rejoin the original path to retrace your steps to the start.

Devil's Kitchen. The names Glyder Fach and Glyder Fawr sound romantic but translate disappointingly as 'small' and 'big heap'. Behind you are the gentler slopes of Y Garn (3,104 feet/946 metres). Along the tops of the Glyder range lie piles of smooth slabs in strange formations — the result of erosion and cracking.

WATCHING WILDLIFE

To see wildlife in this area requires patience — and a pair of binoculars. Mountain goats, for instance, are shy creatures, but impressive with their long horns. Peregrine falcons can be seen hovering before swooping swiftly on their prey. Peregrines fight for territory with the ravens which build their huge stick nests on the high ledges. In spring, the common sandpiper can be seen on the edges of the lake, and in summer, flocks of choughs search for food in the grasslands.

▲ *Mountain goats were introduced into the area by man. Today they are wild, fending for themselves on the crags.*
◀ *The Devil's Kitchen is the dark chasm in the centre of the range.*

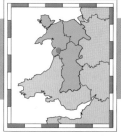

Overlooking the battle site of Camlan on the edge of Snowdonia

▲ *This field peacefully grazed by sheep is known as the site of King Arthur's last battle. (inset) Rhododendrons, once wild in the Himalayas, now grow wild on the Welsh hills.*

▼ *The forest track at Dinas Mawddwy.*

Step into the Celtic twilight of the 6th century, when the legendary King Arthur defeated his rebellious nephew Mordred at the Battle of Camlan.

The battlefield stretches down to the sinuous River Dyfi, and can be seen from a height of 800 feet (240 metres) after an ascent past conifer trees and an old slate quarry. Descend to where Arthur may have received his grievous wound and cross the river where a Roman road hastened the opposing armies. A more gradual climb allows fine views of Dinas Mawddwy from the slopes of Cefn Coch.

The mighty bulks of Craig y Gammell and Foel Dinas conceal a vast slate quarry **A**, where around 160 men worked in the late 19th century,

producing about 240 tons of slate a month. When the men joined the army in 1914, the quarry died, with

the exception of its cutting shed, used to store ammunition.

Nant-y-Gamell (meaning 'crooked

THE WALK

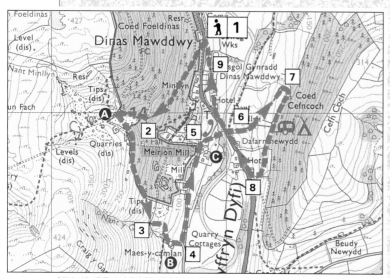

DINAS MAWDDWY-MEIRION MILL

The walk begins at the lay-by on the left of the A470 travelling north at Dinas Mawddwy, between two garages.

1 With your back to the forest, go left towards Evans' Garage. Just before reaching it, turn sharply left up a signposted path to a forest track. Cross this to go up a steep track ahead.

2 When the track bends right, go ahead up a steep path between a quarry waste tip and trees. At the top, cross a wire fence where indicated by yellow arrows. Turn left to pass the old quarry on your right **A**. The fence then turns sharply left and, keeping it on your left, follow it above the trees, passing an old incline. When the trees cease, you have a good view down the Dyfi Valley, overlooking the battle site. Continue in the same direction downhill.

3 Go through the gate and down the steep hillside to a corner in the fence on your right. Turn right to a gate in the bottom fence just before Nant y Gamell flows across Maes-y-Camlan **B**. Go left through a farmyard to a lane.

4 Turn left along the lane to pass the Wool Producers of Wales' buildings. Ignore a signposted path into the trees on your left and follow the lane across a stream.

5 Turn right over a stile beside a signpost. Cross a field to a stile admitting you to the Meirion Mill **C**. Continue behind a slide through a children's playground (which is now a public footpath). Go out past the Old Station Coffee Shop on your left through the main gates. (Out of season these are shut, so retrace your steps to the lane, follow it to the main road at Williams' Garage and turn sharply right to the bridge over the River Dyfi.)

Turn right after the Meirion Mill's gates to take the old road bridge across the River Dyfi, which is sandwiched between the modern road bridge and a packhorse bridge. Cross the A470 carefully and take a signposted kissing gate to the right of the entrance to Celyn Brithion camp site.

6 Go straight ahead, ignoring surfaced tracks to left and right, across a camp site, towards the wooded hillside. Continue through a metal gate and bear left to a stile in the far left corner. Cross this and climb to a ruin. Turn right to a stile.

7 Turn right along the old cart track below the wooded slope of Cefn Coch. Pass a slate memorial on your left, go ahead through a gate and continue along a grassy track through two more gates down to the main road.

8 Turn right along the verge, cross the bridge and turn right at the Buckley Pines Hotel.

9 Go through a signposted kissing gate and up the path towards Evans' Garage. Climb steps and go through a kissing gate to the A470. The lay-by is across the road on your left.

---

stream') flows across Maes-y-Camlan **B** to join the River Dyfi. A local bard recorded the details of King Arthur's last battle here. Mordred's Saxon allies came from the direction of the Midlands along a Roman road (with a similar route to the A458). They camped beside a stream named after them (Nant-y-Saeson), about 5 miles (8 km) east of Mallwyd, where the church was founded by Arthur's nephew, St Tydecho.

SAXON SUPREMACY

The Welsh Annals record Arthur's battle in 537. The internecine dispute allowed the Saxons to recover from the defeats earlier inflicted on them by Arthur and to conquer what we now know as England.

Between 1868 and 1951 you could have travelled here by train,

▶ *The packhorse bridge spanning the River Dyfi. (below) This disused slate quarry near Minllyn used to produce 240 tons a month .*

although Sunday School specials were the only passenger trains after 1930. The Meirion Mill **C** now occupies the old station area. The station building provides coffee and meals of a standard recognised by Egon Ronay. The 17th-century packhorse bridge, Pont Minllyn, can be viewed from river-level by going down the steps opposite the old station.

A seaside and hilltop walk where the River Dyfi meets Cardigan Bay

▲ *The rooftops of Aberdyfi and the Dyfi estuary. The banded snail (inset) is a very colourful sight.*

Aberdyfi conjures up images of the seaside — boats and beaches. A short climb up the hill behind the town brings more than rewarding views over the Dyfi estuary and across the sea. The wild moorland of Snowdonia is also encountered; a reminder that this is still within the national park. The breeze constantly blows from the sea, however. When the sun sets, it is easy to imagine that the sound of the legendary Bells of Aberdyfi is carried on the wind. These are really the bells of Cantre'r Gwaelod, an area of fertile land in Cardigan Bay that was drowned in the 6th century, when Gwyddno Garanhir was the Lord of Ceredigion.

SNOWDONIA'S COAST

Snowdonia National Park offers a fine coastline as well as craggy mountains. The stretch of sandy turf between the mountains and the sea, now used as a golf course Ⓐ, is not

The walk leads you up above the town through tranquil country scenery. This lane goes through Crychnant farmyard.

without interest. Despite being common land, it was enclosed by a property developer in 1900. The local people were infuriated, tore the fencing down and formed a Commons Defence Committee. The whole village turned out to pull down a second fence, to the accompaniment of music played by the Pennal Brass Band, which had

---

FACT FILE

⚹ Aberdyfi, Gwynedd

▱ Outdoor Leisure 23, grid reference SN614959

miles 0 | 1 | 2 | 3 | 4 | 5 | 6 | 7 | 8 | 9 | 10 miles
kms 0 | 1 | 2 | 3 | 4 | 5 | 6 | 7 | 8 | 9 | 10 | 11 | 12 | 13 | 14 | 15 kms

🕐 Allow 2 hours

▰ A stiff climb, but good tracks, although with the possibility of mud near the blackberry bushes. You can take your boots off at the beach

Ⓟ Car park off the A493 near the start

Ⓣ Buses (no 29) from Machynlleth and Tywyn stop near the start. Trains on the Cambrian Coast Line between Machynlleth and Pwllheli in Aberdyfi

---

arrived on the two o'clock train. Contingents from Borth, Machynlleth and Tywn swelled the protesters to a thousand. Asserting that they had right on their side, they demolished the new fencing and forced the developer to give up.

TEE-OFF

By 1927 the land was being used by the Aberdyfi Golf Club. They found membership was declining because golf was played on Sundays up the coast at Harlech. They decided to introduce Sunday golf at Aberdyfi but thereby aroused the wrath of local preachers. A large crowd assembled at the first tee-off to prevent the golfers desecrating the Sabbath and perpetual injunctions had to be made against 16 prominent opponents before golf could be played on a Sunday without any further interference.

Beyond the dunes Ⓑ is a wide expanse of sand. Clean and soft, it is ideal for children. Out to sea is the drowned land, once a rich and fer-

THE WALK

ABERDYFI

The walk begins at the Snowdonia National Park Visitor Centre near the Quay at Aberdyfi. A large car park and bus stops are nearby, but the railway station will be passed soon along the route.

1 Turn left along the pavement of the A493 (Glandyfi Terrace), take the pedestrian route under the railway bridge and follow the road past the turning to the railway station on your left until you reach Gwelfor Road on the right.

2 Turn sharply right up Gwelfor Road. This bends left and right to climb to a signposted stile on your left. Go over it and turn right to walk above houses and reach a track enclosed by blackberry and gorse bushes. Pass a house on your left and emerge at a metalled lane.

3 Go ahead along this access lane, ignoring a gate leading to a road on your right. The lane bends left and passes a reservoir on your right before reaching a signpost at a junction.

4 Go left along the metalled lane to reach the farm of Crychnant. Go to the top of the farmyard and turn left along a track above the farm buildings on your left. Do not take any tempting gates on your right. Go ahead along the signposted path with a fence on your right.

5 The signposted right of way continues along a faint moorland track when the fence veers right. Go ahead to be met by the fence on your right again at a track that soon becomes metalled as it descends along Cwm Safn-ast towards the sea.

6 Pass a cemetery on your right, cross the A493 with care and go ahead through a gate to reach the railway. Continue through a gate, cross the railway at the crossing with care and take the gate after it to reach the golf course **A**.

7 The right of way turns left before the sand dunes **B**, to cross the golf course, with the railway behind a fence on your left. Ignore a stile on your left but take a gate after it to cross the railway carefully, reach the A493 and turn right back to Aberdyfi **C**.

Sheep graze on the lush green hills above Aberdyfi near Cwm Safn-ast.

tile plain with settlements and churches. Strain your ears for those bells, the story of which inspired Charles Dibdin to write the song, *The Bells of Aberdovey* in 1785.

Aberdyfi used to be a port of some importance. Fishermen landed their herrings here, providing vital sustenance to southern Meirionnydd in the famine year of 1649. Wheat and barley were imported, while the local forests were chopped down to provide exports of timber and oak bark.

BURIED TREASURE

The development of local mines was to make the village the port of all of the Dyfi valley, with small boats coming down the river. Copper and lead were found in the Aberdyfi area itself, with the main area on Balkan Hill now covered by residential development. The Corbet Dovey mine, where lead was stated to occur below copper, emerged close enough to the sea to allow direct loading of ore on to ships. At least 500 tones of copper ore were extracted between 1804 and 1863. This mine was sited near the railway bridge passed at the beginning of the walk. The port also exported woollen goods. Between 1840 and 1880 there was a boom in shipbuilding. Slate was carried all over the world from here.

The coming of the railway from Machynlleth in 1867 heralded the modern industry of tourism. The village's success is reflected in its awards, including the Prince of Wales Award for Environmental Improvement in 1972 for its Seafront Garden Project. The Maritime Museum on the wharf reopened in 1991 after renovation.

▼ *Sailing boats have replaced the cargo ships that made Aberdyfi a busy port.*

A clifftop walk where the East Mouse rock wrecked a liner

The north coast of Anglesey is sure to provide you with a view of a ship sailing to or from Liverpool. The port of Amlwch was of the greatest importance in its own right as the world's largest copper port around 1800. Its wealth came from Parys Mountain, just to the south. This association with industry fails to detract from the magnificent stretch of coastline here. The jagged rocks demand a price for their features, wrecking a superb ocean-going liner in 1877.

RICH IN COPPER

Copper was of enormous importance after the invention of cannons in the late Middle Ages. The Romans had extracted copper from Parys Mountain, but the whole of this 489-foot (147-metre) high hill's insides were taken away in the late-18th and early-19th centuries.

FACT FILE

⚹ Amlwch, Anglesey, Gwynedd

▭ Pathfinder 733 (SH 29/39/49), grid reference SH 444939

miles 0 1 2 3 4 5 6 7 8 9 10 miles
kms 0 1 2 3 4 5 6 7 8 9 10 11 12 13 14 15 kms

◔ Allow 1½ hours

▬ Easy, although the clifftop path is stony and boggy in places

P Car park at Kwiksave, Amlwch, or at Stage 2

T Bus nos 32, 62 and 63 from Bangor and nos 60 and 61 from Holyhead, where there are railway stations, stop outside Kwiksave in Amlwch. Tel. (0891) 910910 for details

🍴 Amlwch

At their peak, the mines produced 44,000 tons of ore a year.

The tiny fishing hamlet of Amlwch Ⓐ became a town with 6,000 people — served by 1,025 ale-houses. Copper was shipped from

▲ *The walk leads down a rocky, railed path, next to a sheer cliff to a sheltered inlet, which opens out into Bull Bay. The sea splenwort (inset) is a native fern found in rock crevices.*

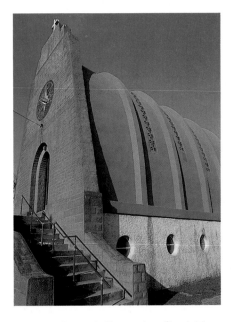

▲ *A sea-faring influence is reflected in the design of the Catholic church, built in the shape of an upturned boat.*

THE WALK

AMLWCH – BULL BAY – AMLWCH

The walk begins from the bus stop outside Kwiksave in Amlwch Ⓐ on the Isle of Anglesey. There is a car park here and another car park at Stage 2.

▶ **1** With your back to Kwiksave, go right up Madyn Road to Queen Street. Turn right, passing the Queen's Head on the corner. Pass St Elen's church Ⓑ on your right and fork left.

▶ **2** Turn left to pass a car park on your right. Cross a road and go ahead towards a school. Turn left just before it to pass a football pitch on your left and the school on your right.

▶ **3** Go ahead over a stile beside a gate and along a grassy track for 50 yards (45 metres), then bear left down a narrow path between gorse bushes towards a bungalow. Walk with a fence on your left and the gorse bushes on your right. Pass the Catholic church Ⓒ on your left. Continue over a stile in the corner, pass a

plantation of conifer trees on your left and go ahead through a kissing gate. Follow a path to a lane.

▶ **4** Turn right to follow the lane towards the sea. At the end of the lane, bear left through a kissing gate to take the signposted Coastal Footpath down to a creek. Do not cross the stream to take the inviting steps up the other side!

▶ **5** Turn right, keeping the stream on your left. Continue along a clifftop path above Bull Bay. Ignore a kissing gate in the fence on your right.

▶ **6** Reach steps down to the beach on your left. They provide a worthwhile diversion. Continue walking along the clifftop path, through purple heather and with a wall on your right. East Mouse Ⓓ can be seen offshore ahead. Do not take the unofficial path across a wall ahead, but go left to follow the wall around on your right. Walk with the sea on your left towards the chemical works.

▶ **7** When the wall turns inland, go right, but veer

slightly left, with the path, towards a wall. Turn right to put the wall on your left and come to a corner.

▶ **8** Turn left up a walled path. Continue through a kissing gate beside another gate to pass Costog Fawr Cottage on your right. Follow the track, ignoring the signposted Coastal Footpath on your right.

▶ **9** Go ahead across a road, noticing the railway crossing Ⓔ further up on the left. Reach a second road, where you turn right. Pass a church on your right and continue to St Elen's church. Turn left along Queen's Street, turn left at the Queen's Head and return to the bus stop at the start.

◀ *Some of the oldest geological rock formations in the world can be seen along the Anglesey coastline.*

Not far away, just offshore, lies the wreck of a fine ship. This was the *Dakota*. Built at Newcastle in 1874, this steamer was intended to challenge for the Blue Riband (the coveted award given to a passenger vessel making the Atlantic crossing in the shortest time). Her boilers proved unfit for the task, but she was heading for New York from Liverpool when disaster struck on 9th May 1877.

The 4,332 ton liner was steaming at 14 knots, 2 miles (3 km) offshore, when the course was changed to take her further from land. Instead, her steering sent her in the opposite

its port to all parts. The resulting prosperity was reflected in the construction of St Elen's church Ⓑ by the Parys Mines Company in 1800. It contrasts with the modern Catholic church Ⓒ, which is built in the shape of an upturned boat.

direction and the *Dakota* was wrecked by rocks between the chemical works and East Mouse Ⓓ. The 218 passengers were soon rescued in a series of trips by the Bull Bay lifeboat. They were followed by the mail being carried to America and much of the 2,000 tons of general cargo. The iron hull had to be abandoned, however, and the wreck is now a favourite site for divers.

Returning to Amlwch, notice the railway crossing Ⓔ. This line was built in 1866 as the Anglesey Central Railway from Gaerwen, on the main line, to Amlwch (a distance of 19 miles or 30.4 km). Sadly, the line was closed to passengers in 1964, but there is some hope for the restoration of passenger services in the future.

A walk above and around a lake at the foot of Cadair Idris

Enchanting views from both lakeside and ridge offer the prospect of magical reflections of the surrounding mountains in a long, rift valley lake on this walk, which is rich in both scenery and wildlife. Like Llyn Tegid at the Bala end of this geological fault, the lake has a legend of a monster. In 1981 it certainly had an aggrieved swan, known locally as Harry. Harry's mate was killed by vandals and his subsequent vicious attacks on humans made national headlines, finally causing his removal to a bird sanctuary. Now, however, peace and tranquillity are the order for this walk, with a hint of Welsh magic thrown in for good measure.

▶ *The church of St Mary at Tal-y-llyn, which dates from the 13th century, stands on an ancient prehistoric site — directly on the route of a female ley line.*

St Mary's Church Ⓐ stands on an ancient site. Part of the present building dates back to the 13th century, with interesting, old, painted panels above the altar. There are also two very old fonts and some interesting graves outside.

It is the site and the name of the

▲ *Tal-y-llyn Lake is a magical place, with no sign of the monster that supposedly ate a swimmer in the 19th century. The pochard (inset) favours lakes with reed-beds and other tall vegetation.*

FACT FILE

☀ Tal-y-llyn Lake, just off the B4405, 7 miles (11 km) north-west of Machynlleth, Snowdonia National Park, Gwynedd

▭ Outdoor Leisure Map 23, grid reference SH 710094

miles 0 1 2 3 4 5 6 7 8 9 10 miles
kms 0 1 2 3 4 5 6 7 8 9 10 11 12 13 14 15 kms

◔ Allow 2 hours

▬ Good paths with a moderate climb. Walking shoes are recommended

P Near the lakeside at Tal-y-Llyn

T Bus no 30 between Minfford and Tywyn

▤ At the Pen-y-bont Hotel and the Ty'n-y-cornel

THE WALK

TAL-Y-LLYN LAKE

The walk starts from St Mary's Church, in Tal-y-llyn, opposite which is space for parking cars. This is beside the B4405, 1 mile (1.6 km) west of its junction with the A487 at Minfford.

1 Take the lane opposite St Mary's Church **A**, passing the Pen-y-bont Hotel and Restaurant on your left. Walk along with the lake **B** on your right. Approach a house called 'Yr Hen Reithordy' and turn sharply left through a gate, following a signposted bridleway. This leads past the foot of some mixed woodland on your right towards the road. Just before it, fork right up through the trees.

2 Turn sharply right at a path junction. Climb above the trees to a track, ignoring a track going down into the trees on your right before it. Turn right through a gate and up the track to a farm. Tal-y-llyn Lake is below on your right. Pass the farmhouse (Rhiwogof) on your right, then take a waymarked gate on your left. Ignore a gate and waymarked stile on your left just after it.

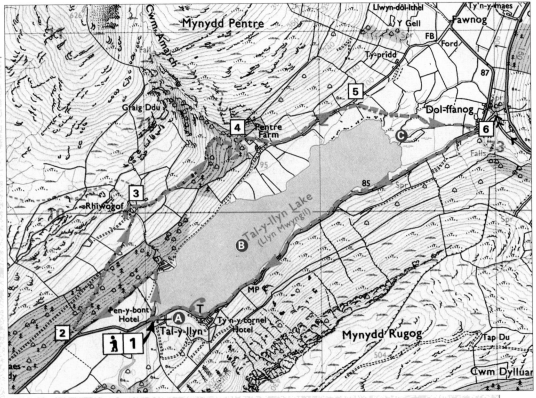

3 Walk with a fence on your left and overlooking the lake on your right. Your path is joined by a fence coming from your right. Descend through a waymarked gate ahead. The track approaches a deep valley. Turn right as indicated by a yellow waymark arrow on a tree beside a large stone. Descend beside trees on your left to a waymarked path, along which you turn sharply left.

4 Cross a footbridge over a stream and go through a waymarked gate. Pass above the farmhouse at Pentre, then descend to a lane that goes along the valley floor. Turn left and go along this lane for about 600 yards (540 metres).

5 Fork right along a signposted path. Follow this over a footbridge and veer left as waymarked. Cross the valley floor, guided by a waymark post. Cross another footbridge near the corner of the field and veer even further left across the next field, as waymarked. Cross a stile followed by a little footbridge and walk around the marshland **C** on your right to a waymark post. Veer right to a stile beside a signpost. Go ahead across this to walk beside a fence on your right towards a white house. Turn right at a signpost, cross a footbridge and a ladder stile and follow a fence on your right. Go ahead over a stile beside a signpost to the left of a low farm building.

6 Turn right along the road. Pass the lake on your right and return to Tal-y-llyn's church on your left.

▲*The route takes you through marshland and over several footbridges, which cross the streams that feed Tal-y-llyn Lake.*

church that are the most interesting. The Cadair Idris and Tal-y-llyn Lake area is magical, with stories of strange lights. Enormous skeletons were found near here in 1684, giving substance to the tales of giants.

MAGIC LINES

Hazel rods were found with the bones. It is not clear whether these were for dowsing and the skeletons the remains of the dodmen who surveyed the ley lines (straight lines in the landscape) in prehistoric times. Dowsers now find that ley lines have male and female lines coiled around them. Female lines are marked by churches dedicated to St Mary, as here, and not far away is St Michael's, marking the male line. The two cross at Devil's Rock, once famous for fertility rites.

The proper Welsh name for the lake **B** is Llyn Mwyngil, which means 'pleasant, enjoyable lake, with a maidenly sense' and Tal-y-llyn means 'lakeside' in English.

Look out for common sandpipers, dippers, grey wagtail and dabchick at this end of the lake. Above the treeline, you may see buzzards, kestrels, sparrowhawks and red kites. The marshland **C** at the top end is noted for tufted duck, coot, pochard, golden eye, great crested grebe and cormorant.

▲*Near the end of the walk, there are views across farmland and soft rolling hills. A bird of prey, the peregrine falcon (inset) stoops down on its victim from great heights. Owned by the Forestry Commission, the King's Wood Plantation yields 41,000 tonnes of timber per year (below right).*

Through a nature reserve following rivers and visiting a gold mine

The early history of the area now known as Coed-y-Brenin was dominated by Cymner Abbey, with its Cistercian monks, and the Nannau Estate. The first house of this estate was built in 1100 AD by Cadwgan ap Bleddyn, Prince of Powys. It was then handed down, via an unbroken male succession for over 600 years, until it passed to the Vaughan family, by marriage, in 1775. It was acquired by the Forestry Commission in 1920 and renamed Coed-y-Brenin (The King's Wood) to celebrate King George V's Silver Jubilee in 1935.

ered in this tree and it became known as the Demon's Hollow Tree. Apparently it fell in a great storm which occurred in 1813.

ANCIENT ROAD

Also dating back to ancient times is the Drover's Road, which follows the river through the forest. Before the railways were introduced in the 19th century, cattle were moved through the forest on their way to the markets in England, after crossing the mountains from Llanbedr. Great herds of up to 400 used to stop in the valley to be shod in preparation for the long journey. They were penned, brought down with a rope

One major incident in this long history happened around 1404. The house was burned down by Owain Glyndwr, supposedly because of the family's subjection to Henry IV. However, legend tells a more interesting tale. Hywel Sele, the eighth Lord Nannau, had resolved to settle a quarrel with Owain Glyndwr by killing him. While out hunting, Hywel pretended to aim an arrow at a deer. At the last moment he turned to fire at Owain. His aim was true but imagine his horror as the arrow struck, not with a dull thud as expected, but rebound with a clank. Owain, protected by armour under his tunic, turned and without hesitation slew Hywel. He then hid the body in a hollow tree and went back to the house and burnt it. Forty years later a skeleton was discov-

FACT FILE

* Coed-y-Brenin, 4 miles (6.5 km) north of Dolgellau

* Outdoor Leisure Map 23; grid reference SH 748256

miles 0 1 2 3 4 5 6 7 8 9 10 miles
kms 0 1 2 3 4 5 6 7 8 9 10 11 12 13 14 15 kms

* 4 hours; 3¼ hours for short version

* Some muddy sections; one climb. Boots advisable in wet weather

* P At Forestry Car Park at Dolfrwynog

* Ganllwyd: village shop and café

* WC Ganllwyd village

THE WALK

COED-Y-BRENIN

The walk starts at the forestry car park at Dolfrwynog **A**. *Behind the forestry notice board is a post with number 14 on it. Posts such as these will be useful to check your location during the walk.*

1 Follow the tarmac road west, up a slight hill, past a timber yard, to a road junction. Turn left, through a gate and follow the road to a second gate (post 50).

2 Immediately through this gate turn right off the road and down a grassy path. This swings left and follows a stone wall down to where it meets a track at post 49.

3 Turn right onto the track. Shortly it bends to the left to a junction at post 11. Take the main track downhill to where it meets a riverside track at post 10. Turn left and, keeping the river on your right, follow the track to post 51, by a footbridge **B**. (If you cross the bridge and turn right on the tarmac minor road, you will shortcut the walk to the

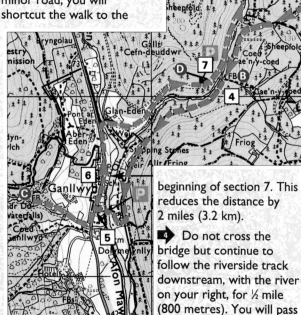

beginning of section 7. This reduces the distance by 2 miles (3.2 km).

4 Do not cross the bridge but continue to follow the riverside track downstream, with the river on your right, for ½ mile (800 metres). You will pass fields on the right and then

a stone building. Shortly after you come to a cottage set back from the track. Go through a gate by the left wall of the cottage. (It looks like a gate to the back garden). Follow the path to a footbridge crossing the river. Make your way up to the car park by the A470.

5 Turn left along the main road and cross to a black corrugated iron chapel. A minor road immediately past this leads to the Rhaeadr Du **C** (Black Waterfalls) 440 yards (400 metres) further on. A signpost to the left leads from the minor road to the falls. Retrace your steps to Ganllwyd Village. Here refreshments and toilets are available.

6 Continue up through the village, away from the falls, and take a minor road to the right by a stone cottage. It is signposted 'No

Through Road'. Follow this down, over a bridge, and bear right along the minor road that follows the river upstream to a parking area. Here is the largest tree in the forest **D** and post 47. (The yellow topped posts denote that you are on the Waterfalls and Gold Mines Trail.)

7 Continue along this very quiet road for a further ¾ mile (1 km) to another parking area. Here the road is no longer

metalled and is private. However it is a right of way for pedestrians. After another ¾ mile (1 km) the track swings right over a flat metal bridge. Immediately over this on the left is a path to Pistyll Cain **E**.

8 Back on the main track nearby, some old buildings will be noticed. This was a mill to produce power for the gold mine. Continue along the main track to where a stone bridge crosses the river to the right. Do not cross this yet but continue upstream for 440 yards (400 metres) to the buildings of the gold mine **F**. Retrace your steps to the stone bridge and cross. The path bears right and climbs up to meet a track (post 19).

9 Turn right on the track going downhill with the river on the right. After a little over ½ mile

(800 metres) there is a left fork by post 20.

10 Take this fork to climb away from the river. After ½ mile (800 metres) you pass a quarry and come to a junction at post 12.

11 Continue straight on uphill. The track climbs to open fields and then on to the road junction at post 13 (on an island in the road). Turn right to pass the timber yard back to the car park.

and then fitted with two shoes on each hoof.

The forest today covers an area of 3,521 acres (8,700 hectares), of which 2,671 acres (6,600 hectares) are under productive plantation. Every year 28–35 acres (70–80 hectares) are felled and replanted. This produces 41,000 tonnes of timber annually — 55 lorry loads each week. However, timber remains Britain's third largest import, mainly because only nine per cent of the land is forest.

RICH WILDLIFE

The walk begins at Dolfrwynog and climbs through the forest towards the Mawddach River. As the path descends to the river you go through an area designated as a Nature Reserve. On the way you will see areas of the original forest with birch, oak, alder, ash and willow. However, as these species may take 100 years to reach maturity, it is not surprising that they have become greatly outnumbered by exotic conifers like the grand fir, Douglas fir and Japanese larch. These can reach maturity within 40 years. In fact, the largest tree in the forest, which you will pass, is a grand fir standing 130 feet (39.5 metres) high at just 60 years old.

These conifers have, thankfully, provided refuge for the rare native red squirrel which has been ousted from the natural forest by the grey squirrel. Fallow deer, descended from the herd owned by the Vaughans are more likely to be spotted. Also found in the forest are otter, polecat and pine marten.

Bird life is rich and varied — goshawk, goosander, black grouse and peregrine may be seen, while pied flycatchers, wood warblers and redstarts are some of the summer migrants. Grey wagtail, dippers and heron fish the rivers.

After crossing the Mawddwy to Ganllwyd a short detour to Rhaeadr Du ❶, or Black Waterfalls, can be made. These have been a popular tourist attraction since the 18th century, when 'rugged nature' was in

Nature Walk

THE PEREGRINE FALCON has a dark, bluish-grey plumage above buff-coloured underparts, heavily barred with dark grey. It has a large, robust body and broad powerful wings which form a crescent shape when seen in profile.

fashion. The artists Gainsborough, Turner and Richard Wilson were attracted to these falls.

The route now follows a forestry trail alongside the Mawddach. The river, like the Cain and Gamlan, is a spate river. It can be fished (with permit), and brown trout and minnows are always there. From June to November salmon and sea trout are making their way to the spawning beds. Spring and early summer also see the river banks clothed with flowers, including marsh marigold, bugle, globe flower, bluebells and cow wheat.

NATURE RESERVE

As the walk reaches Pistyll-y-Cain ❷ and Rhaeadr Mawddach some old buildings will be noticed. The most noticeable of these are just below the latterly named falls. A leat off the river just above the falls once fed a reservoir leading to an iron pipe some 12 inches (30 cm) in diameter. This was to provide power for the gold mines ❸ situated about

▲Like other Welsh streams, the Mawddach is a spate river, meaning that it rises rapidly after heavy rain. Pistyll-y-Cain (left) is one of the spectacular waterfalls in the area. In the past, their water was used to provide power for the gold mines.

▲ *The discovery of gold in the 1880s started off a gold rush; today all the mines are closed except this one.*

400 yards (380 metres) upstream.

The central area of the forest is a Nature Reserve, and the walk crosses it and circumnavigates much of the perimeter. Considerable efforts have been made to welcome visitors, and it is well worthwhile calling at the Forest Visitor Centre 2 miles (3 km) north of Ganllwyd on the A470. Also, four trails for walkers and one for mountain bikes have been laid out and marked with posts with coloured tops. The route covers parts of two of these trails, the 'Nature Trail' with green-topped posts and the 'Waterfalls and Gold Mines' trail with yellow-topped posts. However, these trails are well walked, so our route also goes to more remote parts of the forest thus increasing your chances of spotting some of the more timid wildlife.

FINDING YOUR WAY

There are over 100 miles (160 km) of forest roads and paths to explore. To aid navigation, posts have been erected at every major junction. These have an off-white coloured top and a number attached. If you buy a forest park guide this gives you a map of the whole forest on a scale of 1:25 000. On this map, each post is shown with its number and so your position can be pinpointed with ease and accuracy.

Alternatively, if you use the Ordnance Survey Map, the posts will still be useful as their numbers are mentioned in the directions. Most of the stages make reference to significant posts.

Gold Fever

Mining has long been present in the Mawddach Valley with copper and lead being sought after. However, gold was not discovered until 1853 in the Cwm-Heisian mine which was originally excavated for lead.

Gold is one of the few metals found in the earth's crust in metallic form. It is inert, meaning it will not tarnish or chemically combine with other materials. Gold which has been eroded naturally along with its surrounding rock is found in the silt on river beds.

Panning for gold in the Mawddach is still a pastime for enthusiasts and may be witnessed on this walk. Nor is it entirely unrewarded, but put in terms of income per hour the rewards are small. The silt is scooped into a large dish along with a generous amount of water and, by swilling it around, the lighter sand is washed away leaving the gold dust in the pan.

The same basic principle was still used until recently in Gwynfynydd. An underground processing plant firstly ground the ore to a dust and

This 19th-century illustration shows all the aspects of the work carried out at the Gwynfynnydd gold mine.

then this was washed over sloping tables on which coarse corduroy was laid. The heavier gold was trapped in the grooves of the fabric while the rock dust was washed away. Hydraulic traps and shaking tables were also used. Chemical methods of separation gain a higher percentage of gold, but they involve mercury and cyanide and were not used at Gwynfynydd.

The discovery of gold in the Cwm-Heisian lead mine started off the Dolgellau gold fever. Another rich find was made in Gwynfynydd in 1887. You visit the site at the most northerly point of the walk. In 1888 and 1889, 12,000 oz were mined, valued at £35,000. Clogau was reopened and 20 or so gold mines of the Mawddach Valley employed hundreds of men. Production peaked at 20,000 oz, but the mines closed in 1914.

Gwynfynydd was reopened again in 1981. The buildings that you visit are guarding a tunnel to Level 6. Gold was discovered in a quartz vein that was cut, but not explored, 75 years ago. However, it is said that the future of the mine depends upon its effect upon the surrounding environment.

VISIT TO A HOLY SITE

A spectacular coastal walk along a pilgrims' way to a holy well

This walk could be regarded as a pilgrimage, bringing you within sight of one of the holiest places in Britain. Bardsey Island, or Ynys Enlli, lies two miles (3.2 km) off the south-western tip of the Lleyn Peninsula and has drawn pilgrims since the 6th century. Three pilgrimages across the sound's dangerous tidal race were deemed the equivalent of one to Rome.

The spectacular view from the coastguard's hut **Ⓐ**, where the walk begins, looks across to the whale-

---

FACT FILE

✳ Mynydd Mawr, 3 miles (4.8 km) west of Aberdaron, Gwynedd

⊖ Pathfinder 843 (SH12/22/32), grid reference SH 140259

miles 0 1 2 3 4 5 6 7 8 9 10 miles
kms 0 1 2 3 4 5 6 7 8 9 10 11 12 13 14 15 kms

◔ Allow 1 hour

▭ Grassy paths, concrete road and a rocky path down to the holy well. Walking shoes are recommended

Ⓟ At the summit of Mynydd Mawr near the coastguard look-out hut, or on the grass verge lower down

Ⓣ The nearest bus stop is Aberdaron 3 miles (4.8 km) to the east — for service no 17 from Pwllheli

ⓌⒸ Pubs, cafés, toilets and shops in
🏚 Aberdaron

▲*Bardsey Island — or Ynys Enlli to give it its Welsh name — was a holy destination for medieval pilgrims. Dwarf gorse and bell heather (inset left) are typical Welsh heathland plants.*

back shape of Ynys Enlli, where 20,000 saints are said to have been buried. Their bones are so common on the island that they have been used as fencing material. Merlin is supposed to have been buried here, too.

A HOLY ISLAND

The island's Welsh name is derived from Fenlli, a local prince. The Celtic St Cadfan founded a monastery here in AD 516, but all that is left today are the 13th-century remains of an Augustinian abbey built on the same site. The golden age of the island came with the arrival of nearly 1,000 survivors of the massacre of the monks of Bangor-is-y-Coed in AD 607 by Ethelfrid, King of Bernicia. The island now has five residents, including one nun.

THE WALK

MYNYDD MAWR

*The walk begins from a small car park near the coastguard look-out hut **A** at the top end of a concrete road which zigzags up Mynydd Mawr from the end of a lane serving Uwchmynydd, to the west of Aberdaron.*

1 Look across the Sound to Bardsey Island. On your right is a 500-foot (150-metre) drop to the Irish Sea, while Cardigan Bay sweeps around to the left. Go down concrete path towards sea. This leads to old gun platforms **B**.

2 Continue descending for about 100 yards (90 metres) to a grassy shelf. Go left, walking with the sea on your right. Notice a headland below you. Walk to the next headland and the ruins of the old church

dedicated to St Mary **C**.

3 Ahead is a cove, into which flows a stream. Take the steep, rocky path on your right. Descend with the gully away to your left. This path ends at rocks just above the sea at high tide. Scramble down them, if the conditions make this reasonably safe, to a little triangular pool beneath an overhanging, purplish, rock. This is St Mary's well **D**. Retrace your steps to the top of the cove and cross the stream.

4 Continue along the path which skirts around the coastline and, when it bears left, take it through the valley. This way cuts across to the far side of the next headland, which is too dangerous to walk around.

5 Reach a ladder stile in a fence on top of a low

wall. Do not cross it, but turn left to walk inland beside the fence on your right. This marks the boundary of the National Trust Land, as confirmed by the National Trust's sign

(Braich-y-Pwll) when you approach a road.

6 Join the road near a cattle grid, on your right. Turn left to follow it as it zigzags uphill back to the start of the walk

If you are tempted to take the crossing over to Ynys Enlli, there is a regular weekly sailing from Pwllheli on Saturdays between April and October. This is really for people who have booked a week's accommodation on the island. If you would prefer a briefer stay, ask at Aberdaron or Abersoch for details of day trips.

The walk continues past an old

▲*This walk, which has magnificent coastal scenery throughout, begins with sweeping views of Aberdaron Bay. Later the route drops to sea level, then crosses the headlands (right).*

gun emplacement **B**. Long before the emplacement was built, this part of Wales was invaded by warlike tribes from Ireland — Mynydd y Gwyddel, for instance, means the

Irishmen's Hill. The invaders built Iron Age round huts, and there are traces of them still to be seen.

On the next headland is St Mary's church **C**, the place for pilgrims to say their final prayers before making the crossing. They went down Mary's steps to the well **D**, known as Ffynnon Fair in Welsh. A drink of its water was considered by some to be the end of their pilgrimage.

A stiff climb in a rugged landscape to a mountain summit

Wales is famous for its mountains, but the highest peak south of the Snowdon range remains very little known: Aran Fawddwy, 2,970 feet (905 metres). This is a real mountain, not a grassy hill, so it should be approached with caution. Rock is the principal ingredient in this landscape and the precipice to the east of the summit is to be avoided by all but the experienced climber.

TO THE SUMMIT

Most of your path will be a natural rise, taking you step by step to the summit. The hardest part is the first mile (1.6 km), which will test your stamina, so allow plenty of time for frequent rests. You will be rewarded

FACT FILE

⚹ Aran Fawddwy, Snowdonia National Park

▭ Outdoor Leisure Map 23, grid reference SH 853184

miles 0 1 2 3 4 5 6 7 8 9 10 miles
kms 0 1 2 3 4 5 6 7 8 9 10 11 12 13 14 15 kms

◔ Allow 6 hours

▰ Strenuous mountain walk to be undertaken only in good weather. For forecasts, call Mountain Call Snowdonia (0891) 500449. Good walking boots, a windproof and waterproof coat, spare pullover and some food and drink are essential. Unsuitable for children; young teenagers should be supervised. Dogs not allowed

P At the head of Cwm Cywarch, near the end of a lane from Aber-Cywarch, which is 1 mile (1.6 km) east of Dinas Mawddwy

WC In Dinas Mawddwy

▲*Right at the start of the walk, you will face the steep Craig Cywarch, popular with rock climbers. Common cottongrass (inset) may be found in the more boggy parts along the way.*

by the most exhilarating views.

Mighty walls hem you in at the start. Craig Cywarch **Ⓐ** is popular with rock-climbers. They stay at Bryn Hafod **Ⓑ**, a hut which was opened in 1965. Miners formerly frequented this area. Cowarch mine **Ⓒ** was worked before 1770, but the amount of lead was too small to encourage investment in machinery,

until a London company paid £7,500 for the privilege of raising just 349 tons (343 tonnes) from 1845 to 1862. The crusher house down near the Mountain Club hut still contains its machinery, but the older mines, where the Romans may have extracted lead and copper, are nearer to the route of the walk.

SHEPHERD'S PLACE

After crossing the footbridge, climb the waymarked path to a spot where it returns to the stream. Here is Eve's Heel **Ⓓ**, a smooth, flat rock about 4 inches (10 cm) deep and rounded

THE WALK

ARAN FAWDDWY

The walk begins from the car park at the top of Cwm Cywarch. This is reached by a lane from Aber-Cywarch, which is 1 mile (1.6 km) east of the A470 at Dinas Mawddwy.

1 Turn left out of the car park along the lane towards the wall of rocks **A** at the end of the valley. Pass a signposted path across a footbridge on your right and a farmhouse on your left. Continue through a gate across the road to walk near the river on your right.

2 Ignore the access drive to Blaencywarch farmhouse ahead. Fork right, as signposted. When you are level with a footbridge across the river on your right, turn left for 20 yards (18 metres) then go right to walk with a wall on your left. Continue over two ladder stiles beside gates.

3 Leave the track 200 yards (180 metres) before Bryn Hafod **B** by turning left with the wall, as waymarked. Cross a stile to the right of a gate. The wall on your left runs ahead to the rocks, but you soon turn right along a waymarked path that goes up the valley past the remains of the old

Cowarch mine **C**.

4 Take a footbridge across the stream to continue along the waymarked path up the valley. Reach a fence on your left near the top and walk beside it past Eve's Heel **D** (a flat rock in the stream) and a ruin **E**.

5 You are now entering

a courtesy path, not a right of way, so be sure to read and observe the rules displayed. Turn right to follow a waymarked path, putting a peaty pond on your left. Join a fence on your left and walk beside it,

at the bottom. Just across the fence is the ruin of a hafod **E**, an old summer dwelling where the shepherd would live and perform tasks such as tail-cutting.

Climbing further, you pass Tyllau Mwn, the shafts of Friar's Coat mine **F**, so called by the intrepid Elizabeth Baker, who came here in 1770 in search of copper, but also suspected the presence of iron and

◄ *View from the footbridge onto the waterfall from Creigiau Camddwr — cross it to reach Eve's Heel.*

ignoring a ladder stile in it. Follow board walks over boggy bits past disused mine shafts **F**, cross a stile in a corner ahead and keep beside the fence on your left.

6 Reach another stile in the next corner. Do not cross it. Go right to follow the fence on your left and turn left with it, soon ignoring another stile in it. Continue beside the fence on your left, passing an aircraft crash site **G** on your right, eventually reaching a top corner formed by a fence coming from your right.

7 Go ahead over a stile in the top corner, turn left over a second stile and turn right immediately to go along the rocky ridge to the summit **H** of Aran Fawddwy. Below is Creiglyn Dyfi **J** flanked by grassy slopes **K**.

8 Retrace your steps to the stile in the fence, now on your left. Turn left over it but ignore the second stile immediately on your right. Go downhill beside the fence on your right to a lower stile.

9 Go over the stile and walk with the fence now on your left. Pass the memorial cairn and sign the book at Drws Bach **L**. In the distance is the peak of Pen Main **M**. Follow the path when it veers right away from the fence.

10 Cross a stile in a fence ahead and continue descending with a fence on your left. Reach a boggy plateau where the fence bears away to your left. Go right to a waymark post.

11 Follow the well-established path **N** which descends gradually along the southern side of a valley. Do not be tempted by a private track in the valley bottom. Continue over two stiles.

12 Continue along the path, which soon widens. Go ahead over a stile beside a gate and down a fenced track.

13 Fork right, as waymarked, to take a narrow, enclosed path. Ignore a signposted stile on your left but cross a footbridge ahead to turn left along the lane back to the car-parking area, which will soon be on your right.

▲ *Before starting the ascent of Aran Fawddwy, some boggy parts have to be negotiated using board walks.*

silver, the metals that 'constitute what is called the Friar's Coat'. Iron ore was raised here in 1878 and again around 1910 but the mine seems to have produced little else.

AIRCRASH SITES

As you gain height, the first of Aran Fawddwy's aircrash sites **G** is on your right. The plane, a De Havilland Mark IX Photo-Reconnaissance Mosquito, crashed here on 9th February, 1944, while on a cross-country exercise from RAF Benson in Oxfordshire. The crew of two, including a Polish pilot, were killed. Much nearer the summit **H** a Republic P47 Thunderbolt plane and its pilot came to grief on 16th September 1944, with the pilot losing his life.

MEMORIAL CAIRN

Descending from the peak to Drws Bach **L**, the 'little door', pause at the memorial to Mike Aspain of RAF St Athan mountain rescue team. He was killed by lightning near here while on duty on 5th June 1960. You

▼ *A great cairn of stones marks the summit of the 2,970-feet (905-metre) high Aran Fawddwy.*

The Secret Mountain

Aran Fawddwy is a relatively undiscovered peak. Its ridge forms the southern bastion of Snowdonia and overlooks the River Dyfi, the traditional boundary between North and South Wales.

It is well away from the tourist hordes that throng Snowdon yet, at 2,970 feet (905 metres), it is the highest peak in Britain south of the Snowdon range. This fact comes as a surprise to many who assume that Cadair Idris, at 2,928 feet

On the way down from the summit near Drws Bach is the memorial cairn to Mike Aspain, with a charity box and book.

(893 metres), must be the highest in this area.

Access agreements have led to the paths here being waymarked and having stiles erected across fences that are in the way. This is sheep pasture and it is important to observe the 'no dogs' notices at the start of the access paths.

Convenient fences actually make this route an easy one for the navigator. The magnificent view from the summit is well worth the effort of the climb. Cadair Idris, the Rhinogs, Snowdon, Arenig Fawr, Bala Lake, the Berwyns and Pumlumon can all be seen.

Notice the great cairn of stones at the summit of Aran Fawddwy. Tradition states that it was built by the men of Dinas Mawddwy when they were informed that Cadair Idris was marginally higher than their beloved Aran. In fact, they had 43 feet (13 metres) to spare!

On the very top you will see a triangulation point erected by the Ordnance Survey. These 4-feet- (1.2-metre-) high weathered concrete structures are erected at a point whose position and height is precisely known, so that accurate observations can be made from them for surveying purposes.

▲Towards the end of the walk, the path forms part of the Dyfi Valley Way and leads through lush grassland.

This return route from Aran Fawddwy's summit to Cwm Cywarch **N** is part of the Dyfi Valley Way, a 108-mile (174-km) walking route leading from Aberdyfi over the Arans (the word Aran is Welsh for 'high place'), coming back to the sea at Borth. It is waymarked in places by a special salmon symbol formed by the initials DVW.

are invited to open the heavy box at the base of the cairn to sign the book and leave a few coins for charity. On your left, admire the view of Aran Fawddwy and Creiglyn Dyfi **J** — the lake that is the source of the River Dyfi.

SLENDER TOP

Beyond the lake, notice the grassy slopes of Erw y Ddafad-ddu **K**. These were the home of a black sheep that gained fame by turning up again some months after it had been taken to market and sold in England. On your right can be seen the pencil-thin peak of Pen Main **M**, literally 'Slender Top'.

▶ Flanked by grassy slopes, Creiglyn Dyfi nestles against the impressive face of mount Aran Fawddwy.

◄*The copper mine's crushing and preparation plant now stands in ruins. It was once fed with ore by an aerial ropeway. The curlew (inset) breeds on boggy moorland and upland pastures.*

deposits on the outcrops were exploited. Throughout the 19th century the mine changed hands as copper prices fluctuated. It was finally closed in 1903, when all of the machinery was recovered.

The hillside remained desolate until 1958 when it came to life with the filming of *The Inn of the Sixth Happiness*, starring Curt Jurgens, Ingrid Bergman and Robert Donat.

In 1983, work began to restore the mine and reopen it as a tourist attraction. Since it opened in 1986, the mine has won several awards.

GELERT LEGEND

Along the return route, the walk passes the village of Beddgelert. The origins of the village's name are commonly related to the legend of a faithful hound, Gelert. The story goes that Prince Llewelyn, the 12th-century Prince of Wales, went hunting, leaving his baby son in the lodge. He returned to find the house in a mess and no sign of his son. Gelert appeared, with his mouth and paws bloodstained. Llewelyn, jumping to conclusions, plunged his sword into the hound's side. He then heard a baby cry and investigation revealed his son fit and well

▼*The mine at Sygun was closed in 1903, but reopened as a tourist attraction in 1986. Stalactites hang from the roof.*

FACT FILE

- ✳ Nantmor, 5 miles (8 km) south of Snowdon and 2 miles (3.2 km) south of Beddgelert

- ⌗ Outdoor Leisure Map 17, grid reference SH 598462

```
miles 0  1  2  3  4  5  6  7  8  9  10 miles
kms 0 1 2 3 4 5 6 7 8 9 10 11 12 13 14 15 kms
```

- 🕐 Allow 4 hours

- ◼ A steady climb at first, but some rough and wet ground. Walking boots and a torch for guidance through the tunnels are recommended

- P Car park near Nantmor

- 🍴 All facilities in Beddgelert

- WC In the car park at the start

- 🏰 Sygun Copper Mine, open seven days a week all year; from 10am-5pm summer, 11am-4pm winter: Tel. (01766) 890564

Past old mines into the hills, along a river and back through tunnels

Breathtaking views of wooded valleys and massive mountain tops are features of this walk, deep in the heart of Snowdonia National Park. The walk begins by climbing from the car park, past the old track bed of the Welsh Highland Railway, into Cwm Bychan ('cwm' is Welsh for 'valley'). Just beyond the railway are the ruins of the crushing and preparation plant which was fed with ore via an aerial ropeway, the remains of which Ⓐ can be seen further up the valley.

The mines in this area were exploited from the 18th century up to World War I. The ore was shipped down the river until this became unnavigable. The earliest mining at Sygun Ⓑ probably dates back to Roman times when the copper

THE WALK

NANTMOR – LLYN DINAS – BEDDGELERT

The walk starts at the car park near Nantmor.

1 Go through the gate to the left of the toilets and follow the path up under the railway bridge. As the main path sweeps left up to the line, bear off right on a path that climbs to the left side of the valley. Pass some large rocks and keep to the left of the stream. After going through a gate in a wall and following the wall briefly, the obvious path ascends the valley Cwm Bychan. It crosses the stream, passes some sheepfolds and follows the route of some aerial ropeway supports, culminating at a mine spoil heap **A**.

2 Just above this point the valley forks. Take the middle of three paths and continue until you reach a point called Bwlch y Sygyn.

3 Turn right along the ridge to join a wider path through a saddle into a natural amphitheatre. Turn left to climb round and out the back of it. Continue through the gap between two peaks to further mine workings and buildings.

4 Take the middle path down from this point into a valley. The stony path descends through heather to a grassy track. Ignore a turn left up the hillside and carry straight on. The well worn path descends steeply to the shores of Llyn Dinas.

5 Turn left and follow the Afon Glaslyn downstream, keeping the river on your right. You will come to a road-bridge at the entrance to Sygun Copper Mine **B**. Turn left towards the mine entrance. The marked path continues downstream by the main gate to the mine.

6 Continue along the path to a gate where the track becomes a tarmac lane. Follow this for ½ mile (800 metres) to where it crosses the river. Do not cross the bridge but turn left over a wall stile and continue along a path with the river on your right. Do not cross the next bridge but continue along the river bank.

7 You come to a footbridge; cross this to Beddgelert and a path on the opposite bank of the river. Follow the riverside footpath, with the river on your left now, to Gelert's Grave **C**, which is a short walk off to the right. Retrace your steps to the riverside path and continue downstream to a footbridge over the river. This is on a disused girder railway bridge.

8 Cross to the other bank and continue downstream along the disused railway track bed. Go through three tunnels. The third and longest is reasonably level. (It appears to be longer than it is, since it has a slight bend in it and you cannot see the other end initially. Pick your feet up if you have no torch.) As you exit from the tunnel make your way down to the right, through a gate, to the car park.

beside a dead wolf. Heartbroken, he buried the hound and erected stones over the spot so that Gelert would not be forgotten.

Unfortunately, this story is found in Celtic legend long before Llewelyn and the 12th century. The grave's stones were probably put there by David Pritchard, landlord of the Royal Goat Inn, who publicized the story in 1801. As for the village's name, it is more likely to refer to the grave of the Celtic Saint Celert. Indeed, the second-oldest Celtic monastery, taken over by the Augustinians in the 13th century, was just to the north of the supposed site of Gelert's Grave **C**.

A section of the walk follows the track bed of the disused Welsh Highland Railway. As you walk along it, you will see a machine-gun emplacement between two tunnels. The final part of the route is along the Pass of Aberglaslyn, through Scots pines and larches planted in the early 19th century.

Hywel and hid his body in a hollow tree. Then he returned to the house and burnt it to the ground. Some 40 years later, a skeleton was found in this tree and it became known as the Demon's Hollow Tree.

The Nanney family survived this setback and subsequently gained a reputation for being cultured; they were noteworthy patrons of the bards. The current house was built

◄*The view to the south-west, towards Cadair Idris, from the precipice section of the walk. The rare, nocturnal pine marten (inset) still survives in the mountain forests of this region.*

Along a nature trail around Snowdonia's Foel Cynwch

The route is around the Precipice Walk, a circular Nature Forest Trail with scenic views across Snowdonia's forests and mountains. On the first section of the walk, you catch a view of Nannau Ⓐ, a house originally built by a descendant of the Prince of Powys in around 1200, when there was much ill feeling between the Welsh and their English conquerors. After the Nanney family collaborated with the English, their house was burned down by Owain Glyndwr, supposedly as a reprisal.

INFLAMED PASSIONS

According to a more colourful version of the story, Hywel Sele, the 8th Lord of Nannau, attempted to kill Owain while they were hunting together, in order to settle a quarrel. Hywel's aim was true, but his arrow glanced off the breastplate under Owain's tunic. Glyndwr killed

▼*The ancient lookout point below Foel Faner provides a view over the winding river to the Mawddach Estuary.*

FACT FILE

✳ 2½ miles (4km) north of Dolgellau

🗺 Outdoor Leisure Map 23, grid reference SH 745211

miles 0 1 2 3 4 5 6 7 8 9 10 miles
kms 0 1 2 3 4 5 6 7 8 9 10 11 12 13 14 15 kms

◔ Allow 2 hours

▬ Mostly level, with some rough ground. Care should be taken on the precipice. Avoid very wet or windy conditions. Good walking shoes needed

🅿 Car park at the starting point

🍴 Full range of facilities in Dolgellau. None on the route

WC In the car park

THE WALK

PRECIPICE WALK

The walk begins in a car park on the road leading from Dolgellau to Llanfachreth, just north of Nannau Home Farm.

1 Walk down the minor road signposted to Hermon. After 100 yards (90 metres) take a left turn along a stony track to Gwernoffeiriaid (signposted 'Precipice Walk'). Nannau House **A** is visible on the left. Follow this lane round until you reach a cottage.

2 Pass to the right of the cottage and cross a ladder stile over a wall. Continue along an obvious path to another ladder stile. Bear right to a signpost by the corner of a wall. Follow this path to the right round the top of a field, keeping the wall on your right. After another ladder stile, the well-worn path swings left and contours the hillside for about ¾ mile (1.2km). This is the precipice section **B** of the walk, and there is a steep, but not sheer, drop to the floor of the valley.

3 At another ladder stile, there is a good view **C** of the Mawddach Estuary. Continue around the hill into a valley. The path crosses another stile and comes to Llyn Cynwch reservoir **D**.

4 Keep to the left of the water. At the far end, bear right at a fork to meet your outward path. Turn right and retrace your steps, back past the cottage, to return to the car park.

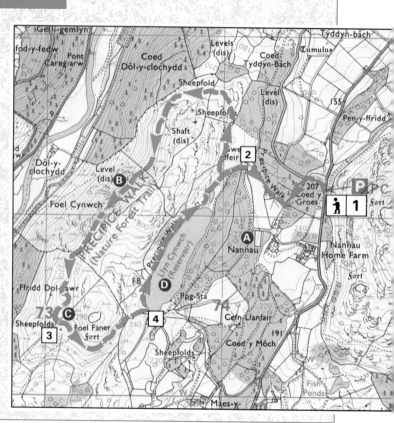

by Colonel Huw Nanney in 1693. The Vaughans, who farm the estate today and owned Nannau House until 1966, are direct descendants. The house is now a hotel.

As the walk begins to skirt the hillside, a forest extends before you. Once known as the Vaughan Forest, after its owners, it was renamed Coed y Brenin (Forest of the King) in 1935 to commemorate George V's silver jubilee. Managed since 1922 by the Forestry Commission, it is

▼*Although now dammed as a reservoir, there is a quiet beauty to the still, upland waters of Llyn Cynwch.*

mainly planted with conifers, such as grand fir, Douglas fir and Japanese larch. The original species were birch, oak, alder and ash, which still thrive in designated areas in the Mawddach, Eden and Gain Valleys. The native red squirrel, pine marten and otter can be found in quieter parts of the forest.

POOR FELLER

Forestry is not just a recent development here. In the 17th century, Huw Nanney felled 10,000 oaks. He was fined £1,000 for this act and, refusing to pay, was imprisoned. He was eventually released in 1612, after

agreeing to a payment of £800.

On the west side of the hill **B** you can see how the Precipice Walk gets its name, as the ground drops away steeply to the Mawddach Valley, 1,000 feet (320 m) below.

At the southern end of the hill is a viewpoint **C** that gives a wonderful prospect over the Mawddach Estuary and the sea at Barmouth. The mighty bulk of Cadair Idris also overlooks the whole scene. This viewpoint was probably once a lookout post; Foel Faner, the summit immediately behind it, was the site of an ancient settlement.

NATURAL RESERVOIR

The eastern side of the hill is graced by Llyn Cynwch **D**. It is a natural lake, although it now has a wall at the outflow and is used as a reservoir. The lakeside trees provide an enjoyable contrast to the open spaces on the hill's western side.

The wood on the opposite bank of the lake is known as Coed y Môch (Pig Wood). Legend has it that this was once the haunt of an enormous serpent that ate people and animals with equal relish, having first mesmerized them.

CONWY FALLS

22

GWYNEDD

Exploring the upper reaches of the Conwy Valley

▲*The old stonework of the 'Roman' bridge over the Machno is so covered with foliage that it has become part of the landscape. The buzzard (inset) breeds in the Conwy forests, close to the white waters of the Conwy (below).*

For most of its length Afon Conwy is a tormented river of white water crashing through gorges and thundering down falls. This walk explores the most dramatic sites along its wildest stretch.

FOAMING WATER

The walk starts at the Conwy Falls **Ⓐ**, approached through a turnstile beside the A5. A fenced walk follows the edge of the craggy precipice, overlooking the confluence of the Conwy and the equally tumultuous Afon Machno. It then goes down to a viewpoint in front of the falls, which are two great gouts of snow-white water foaming down either side of a towering rock buttress. All is safe going until the fencing ends. From there on, intrepid scramblers can get right down over rocks to the base of the falls for a really dramatic perspective.

FACT FILE

✳ Conwy Falls, 3 miles (4.8 km) south of Betws-y-Coed on the A5

🗺 Outdoor Leisure Map 16, grid reference SH 810535

miles 0 1 2 3 4 5 6 7 8 9 10 miles
kms 0 1 2 3 4 5 6 7 8 9 10 11 12 13 14 15 kms

🕐 Allow 5 hours to include visits to mill and Fairy Glen

◣ Very steep and slippery in places. Non-slip footwear essential

🅿 By Conwy Falls Café, Penmachno Woollen Mill Café or Fairy Glen Hotel

🚆 The scenic Conwy Valley line runs between Llandudno and Ffestiniog, stopping at Betws-y-Coed. There are is also a local bus service that runs to Conwy Falls

🍴 Conwy Falls Café, Penmachno Woollen Mill Café and Fairy Glen Hotel
🚻

THE WALK

CONWY FALLS – FAIRY GLEN

The walk starts at the car park of the Conwy Falls Café.

1 Go through the pay turnstile beside the café and follow the circular path along the fence above precipices and then down to the Conwy Falls **A**. Return to the café by taking the woodland path downstream, and then uphill through dense woods, to a beaten way that leads through bracken on open ground to the turnstile exit.

2 Take the lane downhill, signposted Penmachno, crossing a stone bridge over the Conwy. Go on to a group of houses and a signpost pointing right to Penmachno Woollen Mill **B**. Go through the upper and lower car parks to the riverside to look at the mill pond, weir and leat. Enter the mill by the riverside door and leave it through the first floor shop door.

3 Turn left for Machno Falls, pausing on Pant Bridge to look at the Roman Bridge **C**, which is on the right 50 yards (45m) into the woods. Continue walking downhill to a stone house on the left. Beside it is the potato clamp, and across the forest road are the Machno Falls **D** and ruins of the Pandy Fulling Mill **E**. There are two tracks to the falls, an upper and a lower one, and the stone steps are slippery in wet weather.

4 The way runs downhill to a lay-by with an earth surface, from where there is a view over the confluence of the Machno and Conwy **F**, and a steep path down to the water's edge. For a view of the Conwy Falls from an unguarded cliff edge, take a trodden path from the far corner of the lay-by, beside a wire fence into the forest, and then follow the sound of water. Beware of slipping on the soft pine needles. Back on the road, continue to the next lay-by, with a slate chipping surface. Here there is a fisherman's track down to the water. Continue downhill to the bridge before the A470.

5 Cross the bridge, turn right at the T-junction and go through a gap in the bushes signposted 'Ivy Glen. Private. No parking'. Follow the path beside the Afon Lledr to the pool at its meeting with the Conwy **G**, then turn back onto the road. Continue past the derelict tollhouse, and you come to Beaver Bridge at the head of Beaver Pool **H**.

6 Over the bridge take the farm track on the right side of the Fairy Glen Hotel car park for 400 yards (360m), to the gate signposted to Fairy Glen **J**. Negotiate the steps down to the water with care and, if you enjoy scrambling over wet rocks, explore the floor of the glen.

7 Climbing back up to the farm track, continue right uphill and over a stile into woods, eventually reaching a gate onto a small lay-by beside the A5, beneath Dinas Mawr **K**. Conwy Falls Café car park is 200 yards (180m) further along the A5.

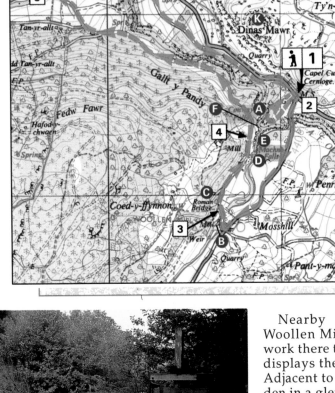

◄ At Penmachno a leat and sluice once controlled the flow to the mill-wheel.

Nearby is the Penmachno Woollen Mill **B**. Just two people work there these days, and a shop displays their excellent products. Adjacent to the mill, and half hidden in a glen, is a sliver of a stone bridge. Clothed in moss and garlanded with creepers, it spans a pretty rock gorge. It is called the Roman Bridge **C**, but is probably much more recent. The romantic Victorians labelled as Roman anything older than records could date.

A short walk on is an isolated stone house on a forest road, opposite the Machno Falls **D**. These falls are smaller than those on the Conwy, but can be approached much more closely. In fact, when the river is not in spate it is possible to walk over the smooth rocks on the lip, and look down the deep chasm that the water has gouged out.

Perched on the steep side of the falls, and almost smothered in trees

▶ *The Machno Falls, though less dramatic than the Conwy Falls, are easier to observe at close range. In a hillside nearby is an interesting traditional potato clamp (above).*

and undergrowth, are the remains of Pandy Fulling Mill ❺. Here woven woollen cloth was beaten with hammers, driven by a water wheel, to soften and amalgamate the fibres.

FLUORESCENT LICHEN

Beside the house is what looks like the entrance to a small mine — except that it would only admit a man on all fours. The tunnel runs for some 10 yards (9m) up the hillside. If you crawl inside in spring, you may see fluorescent lichen shining in the dark. The same lichen is found in the Scilly Isles, but it is normally a Mediterranean species. The 'mine' is, in fact, a potato clamp, or store. Once common on the Welsh hills, this type of clamp was made by digging a trench up a hill slope, roofing it with slates, then piling the earth back on top. The potatoes kept well as they were stored in the dark and at a constant temperature.

There are views over the junction ❻ of the Machno and Conwy rivers as the latter rushes through a narrow ravine in a succession of cascades. From Pandy, the forest road runs downhill through mixed forest. Two rudimentary lay-bys have paths down to the river some 100 feet (30m) below. One leads over a soft carpet of pine needles to a precarious viewpoint directly above the Conwy Falls. The other affords no good sighting of the river, but has a steep track down to a fisherman's path beside the water.

At the end of the road is a charming old stone bridge over the Afon Lledr, leading onto the Betws-y-Coed to Ffestiniog road. From there, another angler's path runs through Ivy Glen, beside the Lledr, to its meeting ❼ with the Conwy. Nearby, back on the road, is a derelict tollhouse; until the early 19th century, all the roads around here were owned by turnpike trusts.

Further on, Beaver Bridge spans

◀ *The arched stonework of the bridge spanning the River Lledr, by the A470, is similar to that of the Roman Bridge. Up the road is Beaver Pool (above), a broad reach of the River Conwy.*

▲Fairy Glen, through which the Conwy rushes, has a magical quality with its sparkling waters and verdant rockfaces.

the Conwy at the head of a swollen section of river called Beaver Pool ⓗ, where cormorants feed. There are no beavers, but otters have been seen, and once upon a time there was a monster with an appetite for fair maidens. The story goes that the monster was eventually dragged out by a bullock team and dumped in a bottomless lake on Snowdon!

Over the bridge is the Fairy Glen Hotel, an old coaching inn. From here a farm road goes uphill, parallel to and just below the A5, all the way back to the Conwy Falls. On the way is the entrance gate to the Fairy Glen ⓙ, with steps cut in the rock down to a great gorge. The walls are precipitous and the floor, through which the Conwy thunders, is of huge boulders and rock shelves. This is no place for the timid or ill-shod walker. There are no handrails, and the path at the bottom has

not been levelled, so you need to exercise extreme caution.

The farm road passes through small, steeply sloping, stone-walled sheep pastures, with magnificent views up the Lledr Valley to the west and the towering rock bluff of Dinas Mawr ⓚ ahead. Then it becomes a narrow path through woods, turning from a grassy to a rocky surface with a sheer drop to the Conwy. The river can be heard, but not seen, 200 feet (60m) below.

ABUNDANT WILDLIFE

Much of this walk is through woodland, some of it planted for forestry. Old oaks dot the open ground and mingle with more recent beeches. In parts larch and sitka spruce outnumber the broadleaved trees, but there is a pleasing absence of regimented conifers. Grey squirrels frequently cross your path, pine martens hide in the trees, and rabbits and foxes abound.

Watch out for dippers feeding in the rivers, and for pied and grey wagtails. Buzzards soar overhead, peregrines nest not far off, and there have been sightings of goshawks. Woodpeckers, several varieties of tit, jays and crows are numerous. It is altogether a very natural, enchanting, wild area, yet never more than a few minutes' walk from a road.

Thomas Telford's Road

The Fairy Glen Hotel was a coaching inn, where horses were changed or added before the steep climb up the old Fairy Glen road to the top of the hill near the Conwy Falls. This is the road taken by this walk, although parts of it are impassable to modern-day vehicles.

Early in the 19th century it was part of the main London to Holyhead road, and was described as 'extremely dangerous to travel upon'. Unfenced precipices and narrow tracks — no more than 12 feet (3.5m) wide in places — led to several accidents. Stagecoaches were frequently overturned.

In 1815, Thomas Telford started

The Fairy Glen Hotel (above left) stands by the old London to Holyhead road. Thomas Telford (left) engineered the new road.

work on a new London to Holyhead road, today's A5. He built in the Roman fashion, with large stone foundations, under-road drainage and a camber. The sharp points of stones were chipped off, and the gaps between were filled with smaller, graded ones to give a level surface, which was then compacted over a period of time by the iron-shod wheels of carriages and carts.

Great embankments were built on the sides of hills to allow the road to maintain a fairly level path; one such embankment of dressed stones can be seen towards the top end of the track up from Fairy Glen. The maximum gradient of this section was reduced from 1 in 6½ to 1 in 22. The poet Robert Southey aptly called Telford 'the Colossus of Roads' for his achievements.

SECRET COVES

Tranquil countryside and the rocky coastline of the Lleyn Peninsula

This walk explores part of the southern end of the Lleyn Peninsula. Lying beyond the mountain fastnesses of Snowdonia, this is a remote holiday area with small farms and a varied coastline of coves and bays.

The walk begins in a clifftop car park situated to the north-west of the small town of Morfa Nefyn. From here, the walk skirts a golf course and goes through pasture to pick up the B4417 through the pleasant village of Edern. On the other side of the village you take to a quiet country lane leading past scattered houses and farms. The lane does not take you all the way to the Heritage Coast — one of the reasons this area remains so unspoilt is that there is no coastal access for cars. To reach it, you follow a wide, grassy path.

At the sea you head north along the coast, climbing through two tiny coves where streams spill into the sea. At the larger inlet of Aber

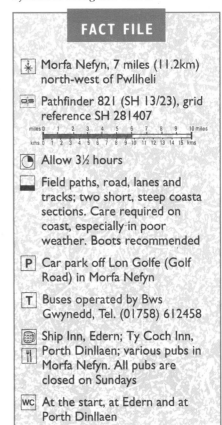

Geirch **Ⓐ**, there is a ruined cottage.

Beyond this point, a path takes you between the low cliff top and a golf course. Plants such as thrift clothe the cliffs, which are a riot of colour in the early summer. Oyster-catchers, gulls and shags are often to be seen on the rocks or in the sea.

THE HEADLAND

Soon you come to a peninsula where you pass between a collapsed cave roof on your right and its sea entrance on your left. On the broad headland beyond there is a disused coastguard lookout. Cormorants fish the waters, and perch on the rock of Carreg Ddû **Ⓑ**. Grey seals can be seen patrolling the coastline.

As you round the headland, the

shoreline changes character, as the exposed rocks give way to a broad bay edged with golden sands. Here there is a choice of path; you can either take a pretty walk down past the lifeboat station and along the shore, or continue along the cliff top; the former route is not recommended in wet or stormy weather.

Either way leads you to Porth Dinllaen **Ⓒ**, a natural harbour that has been in use since at least the 16th century. Sailing ships were once built here, and in the 18th century it was used by smugglers. In the middle of the 19th century it was put forward as the terminal for the rail ferry to Ireland, but Holyhead was chosen instead.

Nowadays the settlement consists of just a few houses and a pub, which contains some interesting

◀ *The view from the cliff edge, looking northwards along the rugged, indented coastline to the golf links. The lesser black-backed gull (inset) is a seabird often seen along this coast.*

FACT FILE

⚹ Morfa Nefyn, 7 miles (11.2km) north-west of Pwllheli

▭ Pathfinder 821 (SH 13/23), grid reference SH 281407

miles 0 1 2 3 4 5 6 7 8 9 10 miles
kms. 0 1 2 3 4 5 6 7 8 9 10 11 12 13 14 15 kms

🕐 Allow 3½ hours

▭ Field paths, road, lanes and tracks; two short, steep coastal sections. Care required on coast, especially in poor weather. Boots recommended

🅿 Car park off Lon Golfe (Golf Road) in Morfa Nefyn

🆃 Buses operated by Bws Gwynedd, Tel. (01758) 612458

🍴 Ship Inn, Edern; Ty Coch Inn, Porth Dinllaen; various pubs in Morfa Nefyn. All pubs are closed on Sundays

🚾 At the start, at Edern and at Porth Dinllaen

THE WALK

MORFA NEFYN – PORTH DINLLAEN

The walk starts from the public car park off Lon Golfe (Golf Road) on the north-western edge of Morfa Nefyn, just off the B4412 beyond the Linksway Hotel.

1 From the car park exit, turn right along Lon Golfe. Turn left along a footpath between the coastguard station and the golf clubhouse. Go through a metal kissing-gate and along the edge of a field, keeping the hedge on your right. Keep straight ahead through two more kissing-gates and across a farm road to reach the B4417.

2 Turn right and follow the road through the village of Edern to a crossroads.

3 Turn right along Lon Cae Glas and continue for about ¾ mile (1.2km). About 275 yards (250m) beyond the entrance to Bryn Gwydd Farm, turn right at a public footpath sign. Follow this broad, grassy path to reach a secluded, rocky cove with a shingle beach.

4 Turn right along the clifftop path to a point where two fences meet. Cross the low fence in front, keeping the field fence on your right-hand side, and make the short,

but fairly steep descent into a second cove.

5 Continue up the opposite bank, following the fence to come to a double-step stile. Follow the cliff edge to the larger inlet of

Aber Geirch **A**. Bear right (inland) to go through a gate in a fence corner, then through a gap in a ruined stone wall. Descend to a footbridge over a stream. Beyond a stone building, go between two concrete posts, then head diagonally left up the slope. Cross a stile onto the golf course.

6 Follow the edge of the links and the cliffs round the bay of Borth Wen. Just beyond the 17th tee, you pass through a broad

area between a collapsed cave roof and its sea entrance. Pass to the right of a disused coastguard lookout and join a broad path that swings right to round the point above Carreg Ddû **B**.

7 When you reach a flagpole, there are two paths. In good weather, join the concrete track that descends behind the lifeboat station to a sandy beach; a short distance ahead, the path leaves the

beach to follow a well-trodden route along the sea edge to Porth Dinllaen **C**. In rough weather, it is advisable to follow the higher route.

8 At Porth Dinllaen, climb the steps behind the toilets and join a service track. At the top it swings left past a large building that houses golf course equipment. Continue past the golf clubhouse and retrace your steps to the car park at the start.

relics and photographs. A popular spot with bathers and boaters, it is an idyllic spot in summer, so much so that a picture of it has been used on the cover of the local Ordnance Survey Landranger map. From here, you stroll along a service road, past a coastguard station, before retracing your steps to the car park.

▶ *From the headland the character of the coast changes, with sandy bays running eastwards past the attractive village of Porth Dinllaen (left).*

◄As the path leads up into the hills, there are fine views over Barmouth and the Mawddach estuary beyond. The wall brown butterfly (inset) likes to bask on sunny walls in these parts.

FACT FILE

- ✳ Barmouth, approximately 7½ miles (12km) to the west of Dolgellau

- ▣ Outdoor Leisure Map 18 , grid reference SH 612158

| miles 0 | 1 | 2 | 3 | 4 | 5 | 6 | 7 | 8 | 9 | 10 miles |
| kms 0 | 1 2 3 | 4 | 5 6 | 7 | 8 9 10 | 11 | 12 13 | 14 | 15 kms | |

- ◕ 2 hours

- ▲ Strenuous climbing. Good paths and tracks over rough ground. Walking shoes recommended

- P Car park near sea front in Barmouth

- T British Rail Cambrian Coast line between Machynlleth and Pwllheli. Buses from Wrexham and Blaenau Ffestiniog

- ¶ Pubs and cafés in Barmouth

- I Tourist Information Centre, near start of the walk

A rugged hill walk overlooking the Mawddach estuary

Barmouth (Abermaw in Welsh) is a resort on the Cambrian Coast that is very popular for its fine, sandy beaches. This walk, though, explores the equally magnificent scenery behind the town, where the rocky hills rise steeply to provide strenuous but dramatic walking and the views are as intoxicating as the sea breezes.

VICTORIAN RESORT

The Victorians discovered the charms of Barmouth when the railway arrived here in 1867. Victoria herself never made the trip; she was meant to lay the foundation stone of St John's Church **Ⓐ** in 1889, but

▶ The rugged wilderness by Gelfawr, marked out by well-worn, dry-stone walls, provides good grazing for sheep.

withdrew in favour of Princess Beatrice because of the intensity of Welsh feeling against paying tithes to the Church of England.

The Victorian and Edwardian buildings of the resort town soon drop away as you begin to climb into the foothills to the east. Miners once made this climb. The old level **Ⓑ**, passed on this walk, was worked for manganese ore. It is still possible to find lumps of rock containing pyrites scattered about, but it is unwise to venture into these dangerous, abandoned tunnels.

As you go higher, you enter a Celtic paradise of rugged wilderness and small, walled fields, and cross into the Snowdonia National Park.

CADAIR IDRIS

There are splendid views all the way along the route from here, inland to the Rhinogs and out to sea, taking in the wide sweep of Cardigan Bay from Bardsey Island to Pembrokeshire. As you turn back to the south, the incomparable splendour of the Mawddach estuary, with the massive bulk of Cadair Idris rising beyond it, is your constant companion to the left. This wild, untamed spot is also a haven for rock climbers, who often swarm over the

THE WALK

BARMOUTH

The walk begins at Barmouth British Rail Station.

1▶ Go up Station Road, cross the High Street and take the back road towards St John's Church **Ⓐ**. After a left turn and a right turn, you will come to a crossroads. Turn left and go uphill, with the sea on your left-hand side.

2▶ At the top of the hill, turn sharp right along a signposted path. At a path junction above the church, go sharp left uphill. After passing the old level **Ⓑ**, follow the path sharp right to another junction.

3▶ Go left along the track, passing a ruin on the left. Go through a gate, then right and left between the ruined farm buildings of Cell-fechan. Fork right between two stone walls. After 40 yards (35m), bear right and keep a wall on your right. Cross a stile and go left, with the wall on your left.

4▶ Ignore the waymarked metal gate ahead, and turn right across rough, sometimes boggy ground to a gap in the wall. Pass through this and turn left along a lane to Gellfawr. Bear right at the house, ignoring the sign to Barmouth, and follow a winding track uphill. Turn left at the waymark along a track between two stone walls. Pass a stone barn on your left and bear right to cross a stile by a gate.

5▶ Go ahead, with the wall on your left, for 100 yards (90m). Veer right to a waymark post and continue along the well-defined track to cross a stile in the top wall. Go right to join a track.

6▶ Continue through a kissing-gate in a wall ahead, and descend towards a TV mast. Turn right before you reach it, to walk with a wall on your left-hand side, to a stile beside a gate in the next corner.

7▶ Cross the stile, go left and bear right to a gap in the next wall, then bear to your right to follow a poorly-defined path with some fine views over the Mawddach estuary on your left-hand side. Descend to a lane and turn right.

8▶ Turn left along the path below the rock slabs. Descend through three gates, then bear right past a seat and go ahead, with a wall on your left, to a gate giving access to the Frenchman's Grave **Ⓒ** on your left.

9▶ Return to the path, go left to descend through a gate in a corner and along a zigzag path to a lane. Go right down the lane to turn left into Barmouth's High Street. Go right, then left down Beach Road to return to the station. From there, it is a short walk down the beach to the lifeboat museum.

---

stark slabs above the estuary.

As you descend again towards the town, there are reminders of a very different way of life. John Ruskin, the Victorian critic and author, founded the Company of St George in 1871 to promote his ideas on social justice. Land and cottages for working men, just below the ancient site of Dinas Oleu (Fortress of Light) were donated to the Company by a supporter.

FRENCHMAN'S EPITAPH

One of the tenants was a Frenchman, August Guyard, a friend of Victor Hugo who had attempted to form a model community in France.

His utopia fell foul of both the Roman Catholic Church and the Emperor Napoleon III, and he came to Britain with his daughters in order to escape the Franco-Prussian War in 1870. His grave **Ⓒ** is located just above the cottage where he spent his last years; he dictated his epitaph to his daughter the day before he died in 1882.

There is much to do and see on your return to Barmouth. Particularly recommended is a visit to the lifeboat museum by the harbour.

▶ *As you begin to descend, there is a good view of the River Mawddach winding lazily through marshland.*

A hidden village amid spectacular coastal and mountain scenery

This is a fairly long, and sometimes strenuous expedition to a peak nearly 1,600 feet (488m) high, and down a deep ravine to the coast of the Lleyn Peninsula, the most Welsh part of Wales. The walk can be made less difficult by splitting it up into smaller sections.

It begins just outside the village of Llanaelhaearn, which has a church founded in the 6th century and a holy well whose crystal clear, eminently drinkable waters still form part of the village system.

You climb a path — grassy at first, but at the steepest part made up of very rough, ankle-jarring loose stone — up the slope to Tre'r Ceiri Ⓐ, the Town of the Giants, arguably the most dramatic prehistoric

FACT FILE

* Llanaelhaearn, 6 miles (9.6km) north of Pwllheli, on the A499

* Pathfinder 801 (SH 34/44), grid reference SH 378441

  miles 0 1 2 3 4 5 6 7 8 9 10 miles
  kms 0 1 2 3 4 5 6 7 8 9 10 11 12 13 14 15 kms

* 6 hours

* Steep ascents and descents. Heavy going in parts. Walking boots essential

* P Lay-by at the start; Forestry car park at top of ravine

* T Some buses Mon-Sat from Pwllheli to Llithfaen

* Pubs and restaurants at Llanaelhaearn and Llithfaen; Café at Porth y Nant

* I National Language Centre, Tel. (01758) 750334

▲*The windswept, prehistoric hill fort Tre'r Ceiri is sited on the easternmost peak of Yr Eifl. Growths of oak marble gall (below) can be seen on many oaks in the ancient wood of Gallt y Bwlch.*

fortification in Britain, and certainly in Wales. It covers nearly 5 acres (2 hectares) and provides wonderful views over the whole region. Some 100 hut circles, arranged in groups and each facing into a common courtyard, are surrounded by large dry-stone walls. There are traces of a defensive stone parapet and walkway inside the perimeter wall.

▲*This track, at the start of the walk, runs alongside a stone-walled enclosure, to the impressive hill fort.*

Tre'r Ceiri was probably first built in the late Bronze Age by the Goidels, and remained occupied through into the time of the Roman occupation. Time and the weather have reduced much of the stone-work to shapeless piles, but given time, if the light is right — a slanting sunlight reveals most — the pattern of the huts and their inter-relationship can be determined.

HOWLING WINDS

If the wind is blowing in the valley, it will be howling by the fort, and the walls of many of the circles still provide much-needed windbreaks. Life must have been hard here 2,000 years ago, with a steep walk of 1,000 feet (300m) up and down to farm the lower slopes, but perhaps the climate was kinder then.

The hill fort occupies the top of the easternmost of three conical

THE WALK

TRE'R CEIRI – LLITHFAEN – VORTIGERN'S RAVINE

To reach the start, drive uphill out of Llanaelhaearn for about ½ mile (800m) on the B4417. After 330 yards (300m), you come to a lay-by on your right.

1 Continue up the road, until you reach a track on your right, signposted to Tre'r Ceiri **Ⓐ**. The path follows a stone wall to your right, and then bears to the left across a slope of bracken. Go over a ladder stile at a wire fence, and continue on a grassy track through heather. The track becomes stonier, and then forks.

2 The left fork makes a wide sweep to the summit. The route follows the right fork, a shorter, more direct, but steep and stony path, to a gap in the stone outer wall of the 5-acre

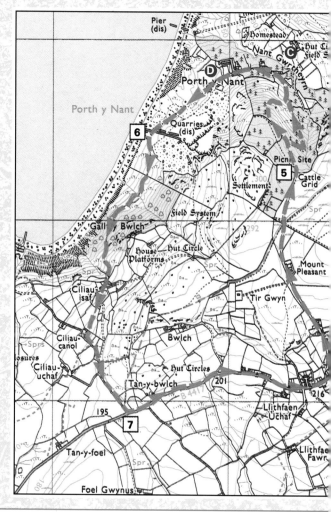

▼*The view from Tre'r Ceiri's hut circles across to the granite faces of Yr Eifl, which are still quarried today.*

peaks, known collectively as Yr Eifl, the Fork. The name has been angli-cized as The Rivals. The walk continues across country along the lower slopes of the central summit **Ⓑ**, 1,850 feet (564m) high, to the village of Llithfaen, then follows a lane to the forestry above the deep valley of Nant Gwrtheyrn, known popu-larly as Vortigern's Ravine **Ⓒ**.

VORTIGERN'S RAVINE

In a castle here, King Vortigern of south-east England once sought refuge after betraying the British to the Jutes under Hengist and Horsa in AD499. Nature avenged his peo-ple; Vortigern burned to death in his castle after it was struck by light-ning. Given that Welsh was the language of the British, who found their final refuge from successive waves of invaders from the east in what is now Wales, it is appropriate that the site of the king's castle is now occupied by a thriving National Language Centre.

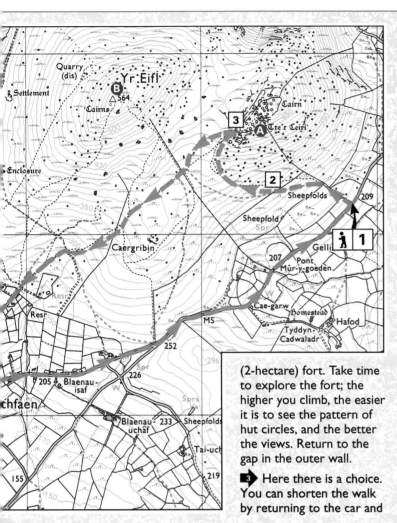

driving to the Forestry car park at stage 5. Otherwise, take the right-hand, grassy path curving away from the gap. Aim first for the highest point of Yr Eifl **B**, then descend gently on a well-defined track over the saddle between the mountain and Caergribin, the rocky outcrop to the south. The track becomes a rough farm road, then a lane, which you follow to the B4417 in Llithfaen.

4 Turn right, then right again opposite the post office. Follow this lane to the edge of the forestry, where there is a car park and picnic site.

5 The lane becomes a well-metalled road, which winds down the side of the ravine **C** to Porth y Nant **D**. In dry weather it is more fun to take the old track that strikes off to the right soon after entering the forestry, and rejoins the new road nearer the

village. After visiting the restored village and looking at the remains of the port along the shore, you have another choice to make; you can retrace your steps into Llithfaen, then turn left along the B4417 back to the start, or continue along a well-marked route along the cliff tops. Pick this up at a point waymarked 5 on the road to the beach. Go down a path to an old incline, at the bottom of which are the remains of a quarry.

6 Follow waymark posts 6 to 10, climbing stone steps and going up a slope through bracken to a junction of paths. Go right to a stone wall. Follow the path to the farmhouse of Ciliau-isáf, and continue through open fields to a farm track. Turn left down the track.

7 At the B4417 turn left for Llithfaen and follow the road back to the car.

(2-hectare) fort. Take time to explore the fort; the higher you climb, the easier it is to see the pattern of hut circles, and the better the views. Return to the gap in the outer wall.

3 Here there is a choice. You can shorten the walk by returning to the car and

For centuries, a community of farmers scraped a living off the small patches of fertile land on the slopes of the ravine. With the coming of the Industrial Revolution, some faces of Yr Eifl were quarried for granite, and a model village, Porth y Nant **D**, was built in 1863 on a grassy ledge by the sea to house the workforce. The village was completely self-contained, with a chapel, a school, a village green and a grand house for the quarry manager.

GRANITE QUARRIES

The granite was shipped out from a quay, and most of the village's supplies also had to be brought in from the sea, as the only other access was down a rocky, rutted path dropping some 800 feet (240m)

◀ *For centuries, farming and quarrying have provided a meagre living for the inhabitants of Vortigern's Ravine, whose only means of access was along old tracks like this one (above right).*

in ½ mile (800m), and impassable to any vehicle more complex than a horse-drawn sled.

Today, the village is beautifully restored, and a metalled road with breathtaking gradients and hairpins has been engineered to service the Nant Gwrtheyrn National Language Centre, which has a café for students and visitors. The treacherously steep and slippery original track, however, is still open, and passable with care, for those who wish to get an idea of the harshness of life here as it was in previous centuries.

From Porth y Nant, the route takes you along a well-marked

▼ *Sheep graze happily by the lanes that climb up to the lush forestry above the deep valley of Vortigern's Ravine.*

▲ *The walk begins outside the peaceful village of Llanaelhaearn which boasts a 6th-century church and a holy well.*

clifftop route past Gallt y Bwlch, an ancient wood of stunted sessile oaks, birch trees and wood sage. The area has been designated a Site of Special Scientific Interest, and the cliffs, which rise some 300 feet (90m) above the sea, are a nesting site for thousands of seabirds.

You pass Ciliau-isáf, an 18th-century farmhouse, and continue on a farm track from which there are views ahead of Porth Dinllaen, a little harbour village that once tried to compete with Holyhead for the Irish packet-boat trade. The route continues on farm tracks and through stone-walled fields to the B4417, which returns you to the start.

Keeping Welsh Alive

Welsh was once the mother tongue of these islands, the national language of Britain. English is not indigenous, but an amalgam of the languages spoken by successive waves of invaders and conquerors.

Saxons pushed the Brythonic, or British-speaking, inhabitants further and further west and north until they were concentrated in what is now Wales and the Scottish lowlands.

The Vikings and the Danes added their influence to Saxon to create Old English, then the Normans added elements of French to the melting pot, and pushed the Saxons north until they swamped the Welsh speakers up in Scotland.

The Welsh National Language Centre, in the carefully restored village of Porth y Nant, once the home of quarry workers, has residential quarters for 65 students.

Welsh had virtually died out after World War II, and was spoken as a first language only in remote parts of the Principality. A resurgence of interest began in the 1960s. There are now more than 500,000 fluent speakers, and many more with a working understanding of the language. Far from being a dead language, Welsh is now a positive asset; all of the county councils feel a working knowledge of it is essential for employment, while in Gwynedd an academic qualification is mandatory.

The National Language Centre was the brainchild of a local GP, Dr Clowes, who helped form the trust that bought the derelict village of Porth y Nant in 1978. Today, the Centre runs courses for individuals, families and groups throughout the year, with residential quarters for 65 students in the restored cottages.

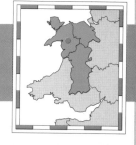

GWYNEDD

A walk beside a mountain stream to a breathtaking view

The Afon Cynfal, tumbling and swirling over its rocky bed, is your companion for much of this walk. At the start of the route, it is like many other Welsh mountain streams — very active, without being particularly spectacular — but there is a surprise in store.

UP THE RIVERBANK

The walk starts off on a fairly well-surfaced road, which, partway up a steep bank beside the river, becomes a rough slate track. The trees are encrusted with mosses and lichens, testimony to the quality of the air. Those on the side of Cwm Cynfal **A** are relatively widely spaced; those on the opposite bank form an impenetrable forest.

The track eventually comes to an

FACT FILE

- Bont Newydd, 1 mile (1.6km) south-west of Ffestiniog, on the A470

- Outdoor Leisure Map 18, grid reference SH 714409

  miles 0 1 2 3 4 5 6 7 8 9 10 miles
  kms 0 1 2 3 4 5 6 7 8 9 10 11 12 13 14 15 kms

- Allow 4 hours

- Mostly easy going with one very steep uphill section and one fairly steep descent. Footwear with a good grip on steep grass slopes recommended. Escape route if weather deteriorates

- **P** In a lane off the A470 at the start

- **T** Scenic railway from Porthmadog to Ffestiniog, 1 mile (1.6km) from the start. Buses from Caernarfon to Ffestiniog

- The two hotels in Ffestiniog have public bars

▲*Part of the six falls of Rhaeadr-y-Cwm, where the Afon Cynfal tumbles into a gorge. The stonefly (inset) lays its eggs in the river and the resulting nymphs live underwater for three years.*

end at the door of the lonely Cwm Farm **B**, which was built in 1492 and has undergone little alteration since. The farmhouse stands by the river, over which two large slate slabs form a bridge via a small island. This is the farmer's short-cut to his nearest neighbour, 1 mile (1.6km) away in the forest.

The walk continues across two fields used as sheep pasture, then rises steeply past a pair of small cascades, and curves around a high solitary hill. On the other side of the hill, a little way to the right of the track, the ground falls away almost vertically into a narrow ravine, at the head of which is Rhaeadr-y-Cwm **C**, a 600-foot (180-m) mare's tail of cascading white water. Made

THE WALK

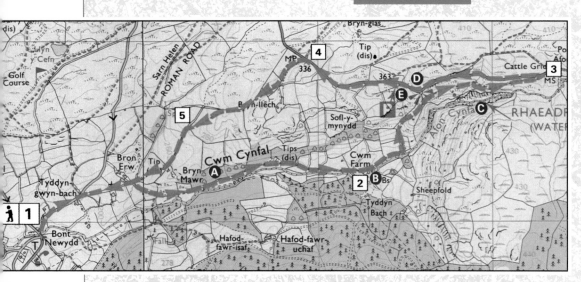

BONT NEWYDD – RHAEADR-Y-CWM

The walk begins at Bont Newydd, a bridge on the A470 south of Ffestiniog.

➤ **1** Follow the little lane on the Ffestiniog side of the bridge, and continue to a fork just beyond a farmhouse on your right. The lane proper continues left uphill, but you take the right fork on a rougher road, to pass a chapel and a straggle of farm buildings on your left. Go through a gate beside the remains of a chapel among trees. Enter a valley **A**, walking a little above the river. Ignore a right fork dipping down to a bridge over the river; keep walking slightly uphill, then across an open field to Cwm Farm **B**.

➤ **2** Skirt the farm, keeping to the field on the left of it. Go alongside the river and over stiles in two stone walls. Strike left uphill. The track here is a broad, flat, grassy incline. Rhaeadr-y-Cwm **C** can intermittently be seen and heard over on your right-hand side.

➤ **3** At a road, turn left and walk past two good viewpoints **D** and **E**. Continue for another ⅓ mile (550m) to a footpath signpost just before a milestone.

➤ **4** If the weather deteriorates, it is quicker and safer to continue along the road, then turn left either down the footpath marking the course of a Roman road, Sarn Helen, or, a little further on, the metalled by-road to Bont Newydd. Otherwise, go left through the gate onto a footpath, which starts as a grassy farm road. When this turns left downhill, take a track to the right across rough ground to a waymarked gap in a stone wall. Go ahead to a stile in another stone wall, also marked with a yellow arrow. At this point, the path turns right downhill. Keep close to the chainlink fence as far as a farm track at the bottom of the field.

➤ **5** Turn left and go downhill on the track to a farm, Bron Erw, which sits at the base of a distinctive hillock. Turn right along the lane you followed earlier to return to Bont Newydd, and the starting point of the walk.

---

up of six falls in all, it disappears from your sight into a rocky gorge.

The track continues uphill towards the Ffestiniog to Betws-y-Coed road. As you climb, you can hear and sometimes catch a glimpse of the waters, but once you are on the road, the walk back towards Ffestiniog takes you past two memorable viewpoints.

The first is a small, stone-walled platform **D** through a gap in the wall lining the road. This provides a high, oblique view of the Rhaeadr-y-Cwm cataracts.

The second viewpoint **E**, a little further along, is much larger and has a car park. There is a spectacular panoramic view, which includes the Vale of Ffestiniog, the sea glinting in Tremadog Bay and the southern mountain peaks of Snowdonia National Park. It is a scene of richly wooded hills and distant craggy mountains, of green trees and greener fields speckled with white sheep.

▶ *At Cwm Farm a hefty slate slab makes a footbridge over the Afon Cynfal. From the top of Rhaeadr-y-Cwm there is a fine view (left) over the forested slopes of the Vale of Ffestiniog.*

In the foreground are the ruins of two farmsteads perched perilously on the lip of the valley top.

The walk continues along the road, then heads across country past another isolated farm, Bron Erw, down to the valley bottom to meet up again with the Afon Cynfal, which is followed back to the start.

GWYNEDD

A ruined priory on the way to a headland above a holy island

This walk explores a historic corner of east Anglesey. On the way, you can picnic on beaches with views across the water to Snowdon, sit on the soft grass beside a ruined priory or linger on a rocky promontory that overlooks a holy island.

Llangoed, where the walk begins, has an activities and study centre, and a 17th-century church. You cross the bridge at the north end of the village and head off along a pleasant path through woods beside the Afon Lleiniog, a small river. For much of the way, the ground on either side is thickly carpeted with wild flowers. Yellow primroses and

FACT FILE

- Llangoed, 7 miles (11.2km) north-east of the Menai Bridge, on the B5109

- Pathfinder 752 (SH 67), grid reference SH 610796

  miles 0 1 2 3 4 5 6 7 8 9 10 miles
  kms 0 1 2 3 4 5 6 7 8 9 10 11 12 13 14 15 kms

- Allow 4 hours

- Fairly easy walking on lanes, and footpaths that may be muddy

- P Car park at the start

- T BR to Bangor. Tel. (0891) 910910 for details of buses from Bangor to Llangoed

- Pubs and cafés in Llangoed, and toilets and a café at Penmon Point, which is open Apr-Oct

▲*Though many of the priory buildings are in ruins, the dovecote, built around 1600, is in good repair. Wild garlic, or ramsons (below left), carpets the woodland near the start of the walk.*

daffodils cluster round the feet of oaks and birches, and flag irises grow beside the water.

Castell Aberlleiniog Ⓐ, a symmetrical wooded hill just north of the path, is easy to miss when the trees are in full leaf. This man-made earth mound stands 30 feet (9m) high, and once supported a timber castle built by the Earl of Chester in 1088. The ruined stone bailey now visible on top was built later.

WILD FLOWERS

The mound is a sanctuary for wild flowers — aconites, primroses, violets, campions, wood anemones and daisies are thick on the ground in springtime, well-displayed in their tiers on the sloping ground. A barbed-wire fence protects them from thoughtless trampling.

After that botanical delight, the walk continues for some way along the road, following the shoreline of the Menai Strait. At low tide, you can take a short cut across a sand and shingle beach. Virtually the

THE WALK

LLANGOED – PENMON POINT

The walk starts from the car park at the northern end of Llangoed, just to the south of the stone bridge over the Afon Lleiniog.

➡ Cross the bridge and turn sharp right down a signposted concrete footpath along the stream bordered by trees. When the concrete path bends left towards a sewage works, continue straight on into woodland.

2️⃣ Turn left by the remains of a gateway across the path and walk a few paces to the bank of the stream. Castell Aberlleiniog Ⓐ lies across the water-meadow on the other side of the stream. Return to the path and continue until you come to a road.

3️⃣ Turn left and follow the road to the shore, then inland to a T-junction. Turn right, back to the shore, and continue on the road

alongside Porth Penmon bay. (You can walk this stretch along the beach when the tide permits.) When the road eventually leaves the shore, follow it up to Penmon Priory Ⓑ.

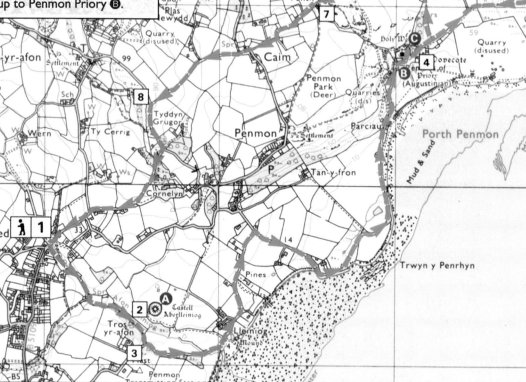

magnificent, both at high tide, looking across 10 miles (16km) of water, and at low tide, when much of that distance is covered by glistening wet sand. Those who love to watch

◀ *An 11th-century wooden castle stood on the man-made mound of Castell Aberlleiniog. Porth Penmon (below) is a shingle cove beneath the priory.*

whole length of the Snowdonia range is visible across the strait. You may just discern the peak of Snowdon itself, though this is best seen at dawn, when the sun looms up from behind the mountains, or at sunset, when the mountains are warmly lit from the front.

The expansive views also take in Great Ormes Head. The scene is

boats sailing to and fro should make this walk on a summer's weekend or in the first week of August, when the Menai Strait Regatta takes place.

Leaving the beach and moving inland, the route reaches the cluster of ancient buildings around Penmon Priory Ⓑ, which St Cynlas founded in the 6th century and later gave to his brother St Seiriol. It was largely

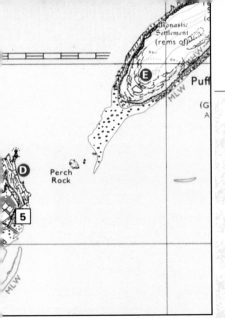

Puffin Island **E**.

5 ➤ Retrace your steps uphill. About 300 yards (270m) before the dovecote, there is a metal gate on your right. Go through the gate to the far left-hand corner of the field, where there are some cattle pens.

6 ➤ Continue straight ahead into another field. Turn immediately left to follow the high stone wall of the deer park on your left uphill towards a white cottage **F** in the extreme left corner of the field.

7 ➤ Go through a kissing-gate beside the cottage. Walk down the lane, past several more white cottages, and keep straight on past a turning to Caim. Eventually, you reach a T-junction.

8 ➤ Turn left downhill. Take the first right turn downhill, and follow the lane back to the starting point of the walk.

After visiting the priory ruins and dovecote, follow the path opposite the dovecote round the wall of the graveyard and past the monks' fish-pond to St Seiriol's cell and holy well **C**. A ladder up the rock-face left of the holy well leads to high ground above a disused quarry to offer a splendid view of the whole site.

4 ➤ Continue the walk by going through a gate just beyond the dovecote, and along the toll road to Penmon Point **D**. As you walk down, a view opens up of the lighthouse and

▲Impressive from the outside, the dovecote is strictly functional inside, with 1,000 nestholes built into its stone walls. The eggs and plump squabs (young pigeons) would have often graced the monks' tables in the now ruined refectory (below).

church, while an oval cell in the rock close by is believed to have been where he lived.

Being a monastic community, that at Penmon was self-sufficient; the monks had a fish-pond (still full of water) near St Seiriol's Well, and there are elaborate pig styes and a deer park. The large, domed dove-cote was built around 1600, prob-ably by Sir Richard Bulkeley, and is well worth a look. It is entered by a low doorway. In the centre, rising almost to the roof, is a stone pillar with corbelled steps; to reach any of the 1,000 nests lining the walls, a monk would have rested his ladder against one of these steps.

From the priory site a private toll road (a right-of-way to pedestri-ans) runs out to Penmon Point **D**,

destroyed by the Vikings, and rebuilt in the Norman style between 1120 and 1170. The church walls are massive for such a small building, and the interior, lit by tiny windows, is dark and mysterious.

AN ELABORATE CROSS

A roofless, ruined, 13th-century refectory, with a first-floor dorm-itory, occupies one side of the cloi-ster, with later buildings attached. The Church of St Seiriol, which sits in the grounds above the priory, was also rebuilt in the 12th century and is in good repair, the nave and transepts being fine examples of Norman architecture. An elaborately carved stone cross in the church was brought in from nearby fields. It shows Scandinavian and Irish influ-ences, and the main carving depicts the Temptation of St Anthony.

The prior's house is still lived in, which helps to bring this religious

site to life. Nearby, at the base of a rocky outcrop and well hidden by trees and bushes, is St Seiriol's Well **C** in a cell with stone benches. This cell was probably St Seiriol's tiny

where lighthouse-keepers' and coastguards' cottages overlook Puffin Island 🇪 (see box).

The point is a popular place for picnics to the accompaniment of the sea, swishing over a bright white limestone shingle beach as it races in and out of the narrows of Puffin

▼*This cell, known as St Seiriol's Well, is believed to have been the priory's original church, many centuries ago.*

▲*The addition of a wooden platform at eaves level provided extra sleeping quarters in this cottage at Pentir.*

Sound, and the melancholy note of the fog bell, which tolls, fair weather and foul, in the lighthouse a short way off the point.

The return walk to Llangoed is mostly along narrow lanes. You pass many attractive whitewashed cottages with pretty gardens, and there are fine views over the strait. At

Pentir, there is an example of a 'croglofft house' 🇫. These are 2-room, single-storey cottages converted to two-storey buildings by inserting a wooden platform. This upper storey is reached by means of a removable ladder level with the eaves. The name is derived from the Welsh word 'crog', meaning to hang; in medieval times, crogloffts were formed by boards placed across the tops of cupboards to provide sleeping places.

Puffin Island

Whale-backed Puffin Island is 1200 yards (1098m) long, 400 yards (366m) wide and rises to 200 feet (61m). It is separated from the eastern extremity of Anglesey by a sound 800 yards (732m) wide. It is uninhabited now, but was once the home of hermits and, more recently, the men who manned a signal station and their families.

The ground is pitted with rat holes (they probably swam ashore from wrecks) and the rats have virtually eliminated the birds that gave the island its popular name. However, man had reduced the puffin population before the rats arrived. Although the birds' usual diet is made up of sand-eels and other fish, making their flesh taste rank, they were once culled for food. To make them more pallatable, they were filleted, their oil was extracted and the flesh was marinated in vinegar and spices.

Puffin Island, beyond the lighthouse, can only be visited by boat and is closed to visitors during the nesting season.

Thousands were packed in barrels and exported to England and France.

The island has several Welsh names, including Ynys-y-Llygod, Island of Mice. That currently favoured is Ynys Seiriol; St Seiriol built a sanctuary on the topmost point in the 6th century and is believed to be buried there. A tower, which can be seen from the high ground above Penmon Point, a ruined chapel and a living cell with an iron fireplace remain as evidence of many years of religious occupation.

At the far end of the island stand the remains of a Semaphore Telegraph Station, built in 1811 by the owners of Liverpool Docks. It was one of a chain of such stations linking the port of Holyhead (from the top of Holyhead Mountain) to Birkenhead, so that the names of ships sailing past could be telegraphed to Liverpool. It is said that a message was once passed from Liverpool to Holyhead and a reply received in just 23 seconds.

GWYNEDD

JOHN WATNEY

chamber at about 1100 feet (335m).

From the cromlech, you can see right out over the Conwy Valley, a view which gets wider and more wonderful as the route climbs. A short distance on from Maen-y-bardd is a single standing stone **C**, 8 feet (2.4m) high, known as Arthur's Spear. This Arthur was not the legendary king, but a giant shepherd who is said to have thrown his stick at his, presumably, equally large dog; supposedly, the stick turned to stone on hitting the ground.

The route leaves the Roman road at Cae Coch for a mountain track, which climbs back parallel with the Afon Conwy under the long ridge of Tal y Fan. Along the way are many

To an ancient church high in the mountains above Conwy

▲*At 927 feet (282m), Llangelynin Old Church is one of the highest churches in Britain. The zebra spider (right) can jump surprising distances in pursuit of insects and is found on dry-stone walls.*

As the winding lane to Rowen leads the motorist nowhere further, the village **A** is usually found by accident. Once there, it is tempting to linger, especially on one of the wooden benches beside the river opposite the Ty Gwyn pub. It is a picture-postcard village of white stone cottages and flower-filled gardens. Through it runs the Afon Roe, which rises among the peaks and ridges that tower 2,000 feet (600m) above the village.

Branching off the lane is an old Roman road, which rises steeply up the mountainside and heads through a high pass. At its far end is Aber, on the Lavan Sands, where man and horse made the perilous crossing to Anglesey before a bridge was built across the Menai Strait. The walk starts with a steady climb up this road, metalled for a while and then quite rough, to Maen-y-bardd (the Poet's Stone) **B**, a burial

FACT FILE

✳ Rowen, 4 miles (6.4km) south of Conwy, off the B5106

▣ Pathfinder 753 (SH 77/87) or Outdoor Leisure Map 16 Snowdonia, grid reference SH 760719

miles 0	1	2	3	4	5	6	7	8	9	10 miles
kms 0	1 2 3	4 5	6 7	8 9	10 11	12 13	14 15	kms		

◔ Allow 5 to 6 hours

▰ Strenuous hill walk over some rough and boggy ground. Good walking boots and weatherproof clothing are essential. Several steep ascents and descents; ascent totals over 1200 feet (366m)

Ⓟ Car park at the start

🍺 The Ty Gwyn pub in Rowen

ᴥᴄ In the car park at the start

heaps and circles of stones, almost certainly the remains of ancient man-made structures. On all the mountain summits parallel with the Conwy Valley are prehistoric hill forts. The track leads to Garnedd-wen **D**. At 950 feet (290m) above sea level, this is one of the highest farms in Wales and has a commanding view of the great walls and castle of Conwy beside the wide estuary.

SEPARATE WORSHIP

Nearby is Llangelynin Old Church **E**. Founded by St Celynin in the 7th century, it has a primitive dignity. The nave was built in the 11th century, and the porch, transept, wooden barrel roof and part of an oak screen in the 14th century. Until the end of the 19th century, only women worshipped in the 12-foot wide (3.6-m) nave, while their menfolk kept to the raised north transept, or Capel-y-Meibion

THE WALK

ROWEN – CRAIG CELYNIN

The walk starts from the parking space in the council estate at the eastern end of Rowen Ⓐ.

1 Walk to the road and turn right through the village, past the pub and the chapel, to where a lane goes off to your right.

2 Turn right uphill along the lane to where it turns right by a 25% gradient sign. Leave the lane and continue uphill past the sign, then down to a white house in a dip by a stream. Climb again to the 'No Parking' sign opposite Rhiw, which is a Youth Hostel. From here on, this Roman road is no more than a rough track. After passing the cromlech Ⓑ and the standing stone Ⓒ, you come to a house called Cae Coch.

3 Turn right, off the road, to follow a mountain track as it bends right and climbs up towards the crags on the slopes of

Tal y Fan. The track is waymarked and there are stiles or gates through all the stone walls. Stay on the track, which is often wide and grassy; pass to the right of a mound called Caer

Bach, then be careful to go clockwise round Craig Celynin, a conical hill just beyond the last outcrops of Tal y Fan. Keep left where the track looks as if it might continue through a stone wall; it actually runs along the left side of the

wall. On the far side of Craig Celynin, the track leads down to Garnedd-wen Ⓓ and Llangelynin Old Church Ⓔ, plainly in view below.

4 From the church, follow a drovers' road downhill and continue

through to the other side of the forest Ⓕ.

5 Where the drovers' road emerges from the woods, bear slightly left down a lane. Where you meet another lane, turn sharp right and follow it all the way back to Rowen.

▲ *The holy well in the graveyard of Llangelynin Old Church is reputed to have healing waters. Nearby is a fine view (right) of the Conwy Valley.*

(Men's Chapel), which still has its original earth floor. The Old Church continues in use to this day.

Ffynnon Gelynin, a holy well in a corner of the graveyard, has been credited with miraculous healing powers. Even today these are attested to by some locals, who will produce newspaper cuttings in evidence. Outside the churchyard are sections of two walls that once belonged to an alehouse used by the slate workers from quarries further up the mountain. Before that, the building was used to house the sick as they waited for the healing powers of the holy waters to take effect.

DROVERS' ROAD

The church sits on an old drovers' road, which runs steeply downhill between high dry-stone walls and provides a quick return to the valley. The surface is now too broken up to

be passable even by a Land Rover, but sheep are sometimes driven up it, albeit slowly; the gradient is steeper than 1 in 4.

After a while, the road plunges into a dark tunnel of trees, part of the ancient forest of Parc Mawr Ⓕ, some of which is now managed. The road becomes no more than a twisting track, soft and slippery with fallen leaves but pleasantly cool for the summer walker. Finally, you follow a country lane back to Roewen.

GWYNEDD

about 1700 to the 1860s.

The Georgian miners discovered earlier workings, which were attributed to the Romans. Recently, however, stone hammers and bone scraping tools have been unearthed; carbon dating suggests that the mines were in use between 600 and 1800BC. Until this discovery, it had been supposed that British Bronze Age copper had all been imported.

About 50,000 tons of mining waste have been removed, and the old tunnels have been excavated. One large chamber contained a great number of stone and bone tools, and

◀At the Copper Mines, the crumbled limestone is riddled with the tunnels of prehistoric miners. The peacock butterfly (inset) can be seen on the Orme in summer and autumn.

FACT FILE

✳ Great Orme, near Llandudno, 3½ miles (5.6km) north of Conwy

▭ Pathfinder 736 (SH 78/88), grid reference SH 766833

miles 0 1 2 3 4 5 6 7 8 9 10 miles
kms 0 1 2 3 4 5 6 7 8 9 10 11 12 13 14 15 kms

◔ Allow 3 hours

▬ One long, steep climb towards the end of the walk, some steep descents. Rough and stony underfoot in places; walking boots recommended

P Summit car park at the start

T BR to Llandudno. Buses, tramway and cabin lift to Great Orme

▦ Several pubs off the route in Llandudno

🍴 Snacks and drinks at the summit, the Copper Mines, near St Tudno's Church, and at a café near the lighthouse

▥ The Copper Mines are open daily Apr-Oct, 10am-5pm (admission charge)

I Tourist information in Llandudno, Tel. (01492) 876413

Prehistoric mines and nesting seabirds on a limestone headland

Viking invaders sailing towards Anglesey named the mighty headland guarding its approaches 'Horma Heva', or 'Great Serpent'. The Great Orme is certainly an impressive sight, and local legends of deep tunnels cut into the rock have added to its mystery. Recent discoveries of ancient mines have confirmed many of these tales.

Carboniferous limestone, laid down between 300 and 350 million years ago at the bottom of a shallow tropical sea, makes up most of the headland. Later earth movements lifted it up and released molten rock into faults in the limestone. Mineral deposits formed as the hot rock cooled. The combination of minerals and limestone has dominated the Orme's history and landscape.

This walk begins near the summit Ⓐ, some 679 feet (207m) above sea level, with extensive views along the coast. Just below are the mines Ⓑ, where copper was extracted from

THE WALK

GREAT ORME

The walk starts at the summit car park on the Great Orme.

1 Climb to the trig point **A** behind the complex of buildings. Descend under the cabin lift to a clear path and follow it away from the buildings. At a junction, bear right to go back under the cabin lift and follow the path across the tramway to a road. Turn right, then first left to the Great Orme Copper Mines **B**. Return to the road and turn right. Ignore a left turn and continue downhill, past the tram station **C**, to where the road swings right over a cattle grid.

2 Turn left, over the tramway, and left again along a waymarked lane to a cottage. Turn left in front of the cottage and go through a kissing-gate to a marked path. Follow this along a line of telegraph poles, across fields to another kissing-gate. Continue to Ffynnon Powel. Go through a gate on your right, and turn left onto a larger path down to the road by St Tudno's Church **D**. Turn right. Where the road bends left, descend some stone steps and follow the path down to a road. Turn right and follow the road as it winds around two hairpin bends to a T-junction.

3 Turn left and follow this quiet road as it climbs steadily to pass the old lighthouse **E** after about 1 mile (1.6km). Continue on the road for nearly another mile (1.6km).

4 Where 'SLOW' is painted on the tarmac, take a waymarked footpath, Monks Path **F**, that doubles back to your left. Follow this grassy path diagonally up the hillside to a dry-stone wall. Turn right and follow the wall to a corner. Bear left, passing the heath preservation area **G**, then turn left along the road back to the car park.

little evidence was found of modern drilling and blasting. These Bronze Age mines are currently thought to be the largest of their kind in the world. There is every indication that what has been discovered is only a fraction of what remains, and this recently-opened attraction is still a working archaeological site.

SUMMIT TRAMWAY

The route continues past the Halfway Station of the Great Orme Tramway **C**. When the Victorians were developing Llandudno as a seaside resort, they realized that a ride to the summit would be a great attraction. Work began in 1898 and the tramway was opened in 1902.

The line has two sections, each with a winding house. The trams, one ascending and one descending, are pulled by cables. The tramway is single-track, except at the passing places at the halfway point. A more modern ride to the summit is provided by the Cabin Lift, whose ride of 1 mile (1.6km) each way is the longest in Britain.

A straight path leads down the seaward side of the head to the Church of St Tudno **D**, a Welsh Christian missionary who came to the Orme in the 6th century. His original wooden church was replaced by a stone one in the 12th century; this fell into disrepair but was fully restored in 1855.

The route follows Marine Drive around the headland, with magnificent views of the cliff and coastal scenery. Guillemots, razorbills, kittiwakes and fulmars nest on these cliffs. As the walk passes the old lighthouse **E**, there are fine views of Anglesey ahead; further round, the Carneddau Mountains of Snowdonia can be seen.

COASTAL ABBEY

The route climbs back up towards the start on Monks Path **F**, which remains green even in periods of drought; local legend has it that this is due to the number of holy feet that once climbed up the path from Gogarth Abbey on the coast below.

The path ascends through heath and grassland, and as it nears the summit passes an area of heath preservation **G**. Wild thyme, salad burnett and common rockrose can be found, as well as the rarer, limestone-loving hoary rockrose and dropwort.

This abundance of wild flowers attracts butterflies such as peacocks, meadow browns, commas and red admirals. If you are fortunate, you may see the silver-studded blue, and also an unusual small race of the grayling which is found here and nowhere else in Britain.

▶ *The brightly painted cars of the Great Orme Tramway have trundled to the summit and back since 1902.*

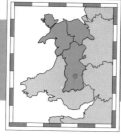

In the hills of mid-Wales above the Wye Valley

This is a pleasant walk in wooded and craggy country with impressive views of the Black Mountains and the Brecon Beacons. It also has historical connections with the medieval Welsh Prince Llewelyn.

The walk starts by Aberedw Church **A** which was dedicated to St Cwydd, a brother of the 6th-century historian Gildas. It is one of the finest churches in old Breconshire. Inside is a 15th-century rood screen and an ancient timber roof. There are two large, aged yews in the churchyard and a stile which was commissioned as a memorial to a Royal Air Force pilot whose plane crashed in the vicinity of Aberedw in 1987.

Not far from the church lie the remains of Aberedw Castle **B**. It is situated above the River Edw, which rushes noisily below through a rocky gorge to join the River Wye just west of Aberedw. Built by the Norman lord, Radulphus de Baskerville, who came over to England with William the Conqueror, it was later used as a hunting lodge by Prince Llewelyn. Much of the castle site was destroyed when the Cambrian Railway was constructed and stone from the ruins was broken up and used as ballast.

A SECRET HIDING PLACE

In December 1282, the English and the Welsh were at war and Prince

FACT FILE

⚓ Aberedw, south of Builth Wells, Powys, Wales

🚶 Pathfinder 1015 (SO 04/14), grid reference SO 078473

miles 0   1   2   3   4   5   6   7   8   9   10 miles
kms 0 1 2 3 4 5 6 7 8 9 10 11 12 13 14 15 kms

◔ Allow 2½ hours

⌒ Fairly easy but with some ascents. The ground is stony so strong footwear is recommended. Suitable at all times of the year except in snow

🅿 Park in Aberedw in the road near the United Reformed Church, on the right as you enter the village

🏪 Pub and shop in village

▲ *These rugged rocks characterise the hillsides round Aberedw. (inset) Barn owls hunt for voles and mice at night.*

Llewelyn was on the run. He is said to have spent his last night alive in a cave now named Prince Llewelyn's Cave **C** (Llewelyn ap Gruffyd in Welsh). Inside, the walls are scratched with the names and dates of the visitors who have been here over the years. The legend relates that a local blacksmith reversed the shoes on the hooves of Llewelyn's horse so that the tracks on the snow

Aberedw Church has an unusual porch made from huge oak beams.

THE WALK

ABEREDW – LLEWELYN'S CAVE

The walk begins from Aberedw village, south of Builth Wells. Park in the road near the United Reformed Church.

▶ Walk down the road to reach Aberedw Church **A**. After visiting the church you may wish to see the site of Aberedw Castle **B**. Go over a stile in the churchyard and turn immediately right alongside a fence. After a few minutes the castle mound will be seen on your left. Now return to the church.

▶ From the church follow the road down to a junction. Keep right of the telephone box and then cross the River Edw on a stone bridge. Turn right up a lane and after about 100 yards (90 metres) turn right again, to follow a rough track through a gate. It rises up through the trees and then bends sharply to the left. Shortly after passing through a gate, go right through another gate on the right. Walk around the edge

of a field and go through a small wooden gate. A path leads a short distance into the trees, where Prince Llewelyn's Cave **C** is well concealed. After visiting it, return to the main track.

▶ Carry on past Pantau

farm, passing through a gate, and after a short distance leave the stony track and keep straight on along a wide grass path. From here **D** are good views. The path ascends through a shallow valley. Just below

the crest of a second rise, keep on the left-hand track, then turn right at the second set of cross tracks.

▶ Follow this track into a small valley with an outcrop on your right, soon to reach a small boundary stone inscribed 'Sir J.R.B. 1882'. Ten yards (9 metres) past the stone, turn right and follow a path keeping well below the rocks. It descends gradually and bends around to a break in the escarpment. Go through the gap in the rocks and on beside a fence, to pass a hidden canyon on the right.

▶ Turn left and follow the fence for 200 yards (180 metres), then go left through a gate to pass an abandoned farmhouse. Cross the small farmyard (through two gates). Follow the fence to the right and, after about 30 yards (25 metres), go through a gate on the right. Head down through the field, bearing slightly right, to reach a small hunting gate. Keep straight on to rejoin the route back to Aberedw.

▲ *The beautiful green fields are good grazing for sheep, which dot the undulating landscape.*
▶ *This narrow entrance gives access to a small cave where Prince Llewelyn is said to have hidden from the English.*

would mislead his enemies. However, the blacksmith then sold this information to the English troops and Prince Llewelyn was caught and then beheaded at Cilmeri, near Builth Wells, on a

bleak December day in 1282.

The Aberedw Rocks are crags which are scattered over the hillside near Aberedw. From the high point **D** there is an excellent view south towards the Black Mountains and the Brecon Beacons looming dramatically against the sky. The rocks are outcrops of Silurian limestone rising in terraces above the deep gorge cut by the River Wye.

BIRDS OF A FEATHER

On these grassy heights there are grouse, skylarks, meadow pippits and wheatears to be seen. You may also hear the piped notes of a ring ouzel or catch a glimpse of a merlin. The biggest prize of all is to sight the red kite with its forked tail — the bird that gave its name to the toy because of its hovering habits.

much-altered church was chosen as the cathedral of the new diocese of Swansea and Brecon.

Of special interest inside the cathedral is an ancient, curiously ornamented font and a cresset stone. This is a stone slab 6 inches (15 cm) thick with 30 hollows cut into it. These were filled with oil or grease to provide lights. It is the finest example of such a medieval lamp that has ever been found.

BEAUTIFUL BEECHES

The nave of the cathedral is 107 feet (40 metres) long and on either side are transepts. The one on the north is called Battle Chapel and was used by the people who lived in the hamlet of Battle just outside Brecon, and named after Battle Abbey in Sussex. The chapel on the south side is called Capel di Cochaid, or the Chapel of the Red-haired Men, and this is believed to be the burial

Through wooded groves to the historical hamlet of Llanddew

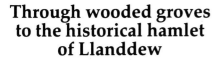

▲ *The River Honddu flows by Brecon Castle, built by the Normans in 1091 and now set in the grounds of a hotel. (inset) The bullfinch builds a nest of twigs, moss and lichen near rivers.*
▶ *Brecon is surrounded by wooded hills.*

This walk starts from Brecon, a market town once known as Aberhonddu, where a Norman castle stands at the junction of the rivers Honddu and Usk. After visiting the fortress-like cathedral, the route passes through the Priory Groves above the Honddu, which rushes through a ravine far below. In due course the little hamlet of Llanddew is reached — once the seat of the Archdeacon of Brecon.

NORMAN CONNECTION

Brecon Cathedral **A** occupies a commanding position on Priory Hill. Built of red sandstone, it is large and solid with a squat tower in the centre. Originally it was the church of the Benedictine Priory founded by Bernard Newmarch, who was William the Conqueror's half-brother. He marched on this area in 1091 and established himself as Lord of Brecon. And in 1923, his

---

FACT FILE

✳ Brecon, Brecon Beacons National Park, Powys

🚏 Pathfinders 1062 (SO 02/12) and 1038 (SO 03/13), grid reference SO 044289

miles 0 1 2 3 4 5 6 7 8 9 10 miles
kms 0 1 2 3 4 5 6 7 8 9 10 11 12 13 14 15 kms

◔ Allow 2½ hours

▭ Easy, but the track through the wood may be muddy in places so sensible footwear is recommended

Ⓟ Car park near entrance to Brecon Cathedral, or other car parks in the town

Ⓣ Trains to Abergavenny, then bus to Brecon

🍽 Shops and restaurants in Brecon

place of Norman soldiers who garrisoned the castle.

Priory Groves **B** contains wooded walks, laid out 150 years ago, on a slope between the churchyard and the River Honddu. Of particular beauty are the tall, slender beech trees. This wood abounds with wildlife, with birdsong, and with squirrels which scuttle along the branches overhead.

The Iron Age hillfort Pen-y-Crug is one of several in the vicinity of Brecon and it is defined by five ramparts and ditches.

THE WALK

BRECON – LLANDDEW

This walk starts from a car park near the entrance to Brecon Cathedral.

➡ Go through the lych-gate and visit the cathedral **A**. Then walk through the avenue of trees to reach a metal kissing gate. Continue between two stone walls and then turn left to pass a wayside well. The path now enters Priory Groves **B** and follows a fence above the River Honddu.

➡ On reaching a T-junction, bear right and then bear left after about ¼ mile (400 metres) and then go almost immediately right just before a metal kissing gate. Soon to the left you will observe the Iron Age hill fort of Pen-y-Crug. Ignore tracks to the right until about 50 yards (45 metres) just before the end of the wood.

➡ Turn right at a waymark and after crossing a stream, ascend a bank and continue along a path between the top of the wood and the hedge on the left.

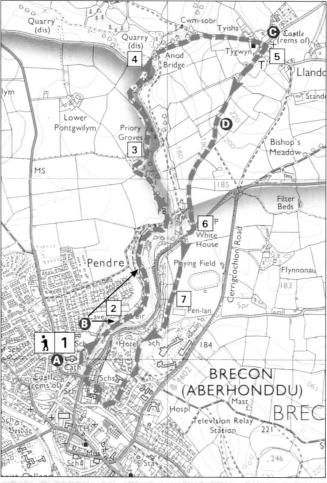

➡ On reaching a stile, you emerge from the wood. Turn right and go down the

field, heading for the bottom left-hand corner, then go over a stile to reach a bridge

called Pont-Cwm Anod. Turn right and follow the road uphill to Llanddew **C**

➡ After exploring Llanddew, turn right at the crossroads to follow a quiet road. On the brow of a hill there is a viewpoint **D** from which you can see the majestic summits of the Brecon Beacons.

➡ On reaching a road junction, turn right and shortly cross the road with care, to go through a kissing gate. Head across a playing field, bearing right to join a fence.

➡ On reaching a crossroads go straight on to the T-junction at the bottom of the hill. Turn right then immediately right again. After passing the school, turn left, and continue ahead down the ancient, cobbled steps of King Street. On reaching the main road go right for a few yards, cross over, then use the footbridge over the River Honddu. Follow the path steeply uphill, turning left at the top, to enter the Cathedral grounds again.

Llanddew **C** is a quiet hamlet that was formerly a place of some importance, being the residence of the Archdeacon of Brecon. On entering the hamlet there is an arched well (Bishop Gower's Well *c.*1340) which once supplied water to the local people. Behind the arch is the site of the castle or Palace of the Bishop of St David's. The bishop resided here when making periodical visits to

◀ *Llanddew church has a 12th-century chancel and an ancient font.*
▶ *The ruins of Gerald of Wales' palace are now in the vicarage grounds.*

this portion of his diocese. It was once the Breconshire home of the famous cleric and writer Giraldus Cambrensis or Gerald of Wales, a colourful character in Welsh medieval history. He lived here for 25 years as Archdeacon of Brecon and left one of the earliest detailed records of Welsh life.

CHURCH OF ST DAVID

Llanddew church is dedicated to St David and it is one of the oldest churches in the area. Like Brecon Cathedral, it is a solid structure, with the tower separating the choir from the nave.

The four main peaks of the Brecon Beacons can be seen from vantage point **D**. These are the highest Old Red Sandstone mountains south of Scotland and from left to right their names are Fan Big, Cribin, Pen-y-Fan and Corn Du.

THE HILL OF LOSS

A walk through a secluded valley with magnificent wild scenery

The Hill of Loss, or Collfryn as it is better known in Welsh, is the burial mound of a band of some 80 outlaws who terrorized local travellers and were condemned to death in the 16th century. They were known as the 'Gwylliaid Cochion', or Red Bandits, and when they were engaged in their reign of terror they travelled all over these once thickly forested valleys, moving from tree to tree without ever having to set foot on the ground.

Vestiges of the old oak forest remain and this is a good place to see many varieties of fungi. (Do not

FACT FILE

- ✳ Collfryn, Powys
- ▭ Outdoor Leisure 23, grid reference SH 893109

  miles 0 1 2 3 4 5 6 7 8 9 10 miles
  kms 0 1 2 3 4 5 6 7 8 9 10 11 12 13 14 15 kms

- ◔ Allow 2 hours
- ◼ Rough tracks that may be muddy. No steep gradients and a flat valley road
- P Lay-by on minor road south of the A458, 2 miles (3.2 km) east of Mallwyd
- ¶ None on the walk, but Mallwyd has a garage with a shop and café

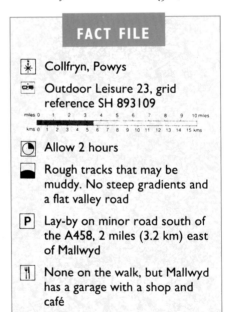

▲ *This gentle valley was once wild and wooded — perfect bandit country. The beefsteak fungus (inset) lives on trees, looks like steak and oozes a blood-red sap when damaged.* ▶ *The burial ground of the 16th-century 'Gwylliaid Cochion'.*

be tempted to collect them unless you are absolutely sure that they are edible.) Located just inside Powys, near the border with the Snowdonia National Park, the surrounding hills are grand backdrops, with the peaks of Meirionnydd in the distance.

BANDIT COUNTRY

The modern A458 road follows the route of a Roman road between Wroxeter and Brithdir (near Dolgellau). It was along this stretch of road that travellers went in fear of the local Red Bandits in the Middle Ages. Fortunately, you can now concentrate on the scenery in this area,

The waters of the Afon Tafalog rush the length of the secluded valley.

which follows two long-distance paths ⓐ. These are the Dyfi Valley Way — 108 miles (173 km) long, from Aberdyfi to Borth — and the Cambrian Way — 274 miles (440 km) long, from Cardiff to Conwy.

If you want to see the burial mound of the Red Bandits ⓑ, which is on private land, go left from the track into the woodland below at a point where the track bends right and a stream is piped under it. The tree-topped mound is impressive when seen from the meadow below.

The end of the 'Gwylliaid Cochion' came on Christmas Eve 1554, when Baron Lewis Owen, the High Sheriff of Merioneth, condemned over 80 of them to death at Collfryn. Among them was

THE WALK

COLLFRYN

To reach the starting point, find the junction of the A470 and the A458 at Mallwyd. Go 2 miles (3.2 km) east along the A458, then turn right down a narrow lane at an awkward bend. Go south for over 1 mile (1.6 km), passing three tracks on the left. Park considerately in the lay-by on your left below a conifer plantation.

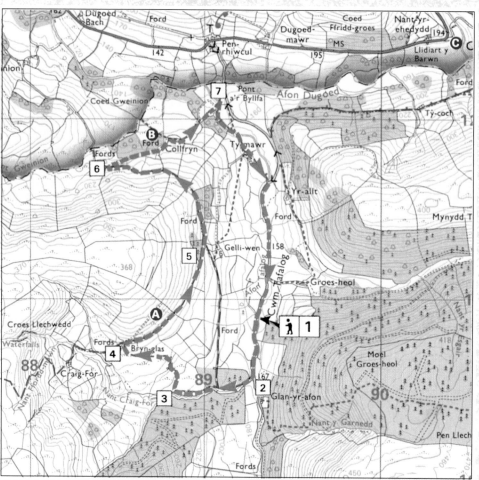

1 With your back to the lay-by, go left along the road. Immediately, pass a gate giving access to a ford across a river (the Afon Tafalog) on your right.

2 Turn right across a wooden bridge and go ahead through a gate to follow a track with a stream on your left and trees on your right. Continue over a padlocked gate to walk parallel to the stream on your left until it bends left.

3 Turn right to follow the stream up to a ruin. Go through a gate to the right of this and turn right along a track to a junction. Turn sharply left and follow a grassed-over track which finally bends right to pass ruins on your right and join a track **A**.

4 Turn sharply right to pass above the ruins and continue beside a wall on your right. Go ahead through a gate and continue with a fence on your right.

5 Fork right at the beginning of the trees to keep beside the fence on your right. Pass a track descending on your right and continue with a fence on your right as the track bends left. Go through a gate, then through another gate to a crosstracks.

6 Turn sharply right through a lower gate. Go ahead along a track above trees on your left, which conceal the burial mound of the Red Bandits **B**. Pass Collfryn on your right and continue to a bridge over the river.

7 Leave the bridge on your left. Carry on ahead through a gate, keeping the river on your left, across Ty Mawr farmyard. Go through another gate on the left to a concreted track. Follow the track across the bridge to reach the road. Turn right along the road to the lay-by, on your left, at the start.

a young man, Jac Goch. When his mother's pleas for his life went in vain, she bared her breasts and said: 'these yellow breasts have given suck to those who shall wash their hands in your blood'.

Baron Owen made the mistake of returning this way from the Assizes at Welshpool to his home at Dolgellau on Hallowe'en 1555. The surviving Red Bandits were waiting for him at a spot where the modern A458 makes a nasty bend, known as 'Llidiart y Barwn' (Baron's Gate) **C**.

Here the baron was ambushed. His companion and son-in-law, John Lloyd of Ceiswyn was allowed to 'go in peace', however. No doubt many hands were washed in the baron's blood — but the full force of Tudor law and order was brought to bear and soon saw to it that the culprits were caught and punished. Although the memory of their deeds lingers on, they have gained a great deal of romantic sympathy over the years. This area was certainly a law unto itself for many centuries.

This windswept track leads to Collfryn.

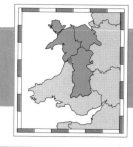

POWYS

A walk along the hills above an historic town

This walk is set on the stage used by the famous Welsh hero, Owain Glyndwr, in the early years of the 15th century. In true Celtic fashion, Owain's Wales had no capital and no permanent site for the national parliament. When Owain called four representatives from each commot (a division of the country) in Wales to a parliament in Machynlleth in 1404, he chose to be crowned Prince of Wales in a moving ceremony before envoys from France, Scotland and Castile.

NATIONAL INSPIRATION

This was the romantic climax of the dream that still inspires the national spirit of Wales — the fulfilment of visions and prophecies. Owain Glyndwr can still 'call spirits from the vasty deep' here.

Glyndwr may well have used the tracks that form the route of this walk, but much else has changed. The difference begins at the Tourist Information Centre **Ⓐ**, where the Owain Glyndwr Institute houses an

FACT FILE

- ⚹ Machynlleth, Powys
- 🗺 Pathfinder 885 (SH 70/SN 79), grid reference SH 748008

miles 0   1   2   3   4   5   6   7   8   9   10 miles
kms 0   1   2   3   4   5   6   7   8   9   10   11   12   13   14   15 kms

- ◔ Allow 3 hours
- ▭ Fairly easy, with only moderate climbs up good tracks, including the Roman Steps. Good walking shoes are recommended
- **P** Car park signposted off the A489 (Maengwyn Street) almost opposite the Tourist Information Centre
- **WC** At car park
- 🍴 Wide variety available in the town
- **T** Machynlleth is on British Rail's Cambrian Line from Shrewsbury to Aberystwyth (with a branch along the coast to Pwllheli). Buses from all directions converge on this route centre

▲ *Llyn Glanmerin is a relatively new addition to the landscape. The lake was created in 1911 as part of an early hydroelectric scheme. The song of the sedge warbler (inset) can often be heard around its reed-fringed waters.*

interesting exhibition giving an introduction to the Dyfi valley. The exhibition would seem to be set within a fine example of a late medieval Welsh Town House. In fact it is mock, built in 1911.

The Plas **Ⓑ**, or mansion, is the real

▼ *A host of royal and distinguished visitors have been entertained at the Plas, or mansion, in Machynlleth.*

THE WALK

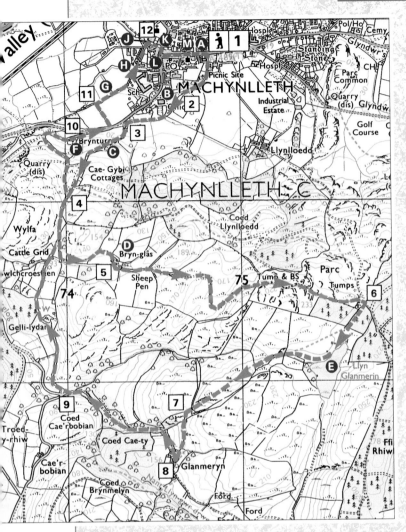

▶ Turn left through a kissing gate to take the signposted path which bends right to go up the Roman Steps **C**. Go ahead through a kissing gate and pass some cottages called 'Caergybi' on your left. Reach a road near a public footpath signpost.

▶ Bear left along the road for 300 yards (270 metres) then fork left through a gate to follow the track to Bryn-glâs **D**.

▶ Continue through the farmyard and go through a gate to walk with a hedge on your left and a stream on your right. Follow the green track through a gate and below crags on your left. Machynlleth is spread below on your left, but bear right along the track before it bends left to give another view of the town. Go ahead through a gate, reach a corner of a conifer plantation and walk with the trees on your right.

▶ Turn right over a waymarked stile to take a path through the trees. Emerge to cross a second stile and go ahead to a lake, Llyn Glanmerin **E**. Pass this lake on your left, then veer right to go over a waymarked stile beside a gate. Follow the waymarked path, which is roughly parallel to a fence on your left. Descend to a waymarked gate ahead.

▶ Go through the gate

and walk with a fence on your right. Go left as the track bends and descend with it to a farm called Glanmeryn.

▶ Turn right, as waymarked, in the farmyard. Follow the farm access track to a road, which is joined at a hairpin bend.

▶ Turn right up the road. Keep to the road as it descends to pass Brynturnol **F** on your right and reach the A487.

▶ Go right along the pavement for 150 yards (135 metres) then turn left to cross the road carefully and take the hedged track opposite towards Tan-y-Bryn.

▶ Just before the track bends left, turn right through a kissing gate to follow a narrow path that was an old slate tram-road **G**. Pass a school on your right and notice the old well **H** just below the ramp up to the school. Go ahead to Poplar Square **J**.

▶ Turn right up Poplar Road (which becomes Garsiwn) to reach Penrallt Street. Go right and immediately pass the Royal House **K** on your right. Go ahead to the Clock **L** and turn left up Maengwyn Street to pass Owain Glyndwr's Parliament House **M** on your left, next to the start of the walk.

SOUTH OF MACHYNLLETH

*The walk begins at the Tourist Information Centre **A** in Maengwyn Street, Machynlleth.*

▶ With your back to the Tourist Information Centre, cross the road with care and take the gates opposite to enter the

grounds of the Plas. Follow the track around to a football ground on your left.

▶ Fork left, away from the Leisure Centre, to pass the Plas **B** on your right. Go past a children's playground on your right and the West Lodge on your left to take the gate out of the Plas grounds.

---

thing, dating from 1653, but with its present frontage added in 1853. Then it was the home of Henry Vane-Tempest, who became the fifth Marquis of Londonderry in 1872. Many distinguished visitors were to find their way here. Lord Randolph Churchill, father of Sir Winston and the fifth Marquis' nephew, was a frequent guest. King Edward VII and Queen Alexandra came in 1896,

when they were the Prince and Princess of Wales, while King George V, Queen Mary and the Duke of Windsor, then Prince of Wales, visited in 1911. The seventh Marquis presented the Plas to the town in 1948 and its foyer houses a fine exhibition of family portraits.

How old are the Roman Steps **C**? Anything that was very old used to be attributed to the Romans and it is

true that they probably had a lookout post on Wylfa, the hill south-west of the town, to which the steps lead. Their main base was at Pennal, where the fort of Cefn Caer guarded the ancient road of Sarn Helen at its crossing point over the River Dyfi, about 4 miles (6.4 km) west of Machynlleth. This may have become the lowest ford across the Dyfi during the 6th century when the legendary land of Cantre'r Gwaelod in Cardigan Bay was flooded. These steps, or the route up which they are cut, may be much older. Ancient Britain had many roads or trackways, with Molmutius and his son Belinus, tribal chieftains, famed for constructing them in the 5th century BC. They often led to mines, like the lead mines east of Machynlleth, which are pre-Roman.

THE NEW LAKE

Local legend has it that Bryn-glâs ❶ is reputedly where Glyndwr stayed during the period of his coronation. If this is so, you may well be following in his footsteps. The lake, Llyn Glanmerin ❷, is not a feature that Glyndwr would have recognized. It is not marked on old maps, since it was artificially created in 1911 for a local hydroelectricity scheme. It blends well into the landscape and can offer marvellous reflections of the hills to its south. Rich in wildlife, it is reed-fringed and provides a home for dragon-flies. Ducks and coot may be glimpsed among the waterlilies.

Brynturnol ❸ means 'Turn Back Hill'. This black and white house is where stage coaches could hire the

▼ *The ramshackle buildings of Bryn-glâs are where Glyndwr is supposed to have stayed during his coronation.*

▲ *The route up which the Roman Steps are cut may well predate the Roman invaders by some 400 years. It probably led to a look-out post on Wylfa.*

extra horses needed to pull them up the old road towards Aberystwyth.

The old slate tram-road ❹ ran from Aberllefeni to Derwenlas, the small port 2 miles (3.2 km) west of Machynlleth. Slate was taken to the

port from the quarries at Corris and Aberllefeni, 5 miles (8 km) north east of Machynlleth. Horses were used at first but, by 1855, the demand for slate warranted the construction of a tram-road. The first train ran over it on 30th April 1859.

▲ *The clock was built to commemorate the 21st birthday of Viscount Castlereagh, a direct descendant of the famous Foreign Secretary who was instrumental in Napoleon's downfall.*

This was still horse-drawn, but made shorter work of the nearly 13 miles (20.8 km) from the quarry at Aberllefeni down to the quay at Derwenlas. However, only four years later the route was made obsolete by the opening of the steam railway between Machynlleth and Newtown. The section north of Machynlleth was used by steam engines to haul slate down to the main line at Machynlleth, but the port at Derwenlas lost its traffic.

Pause when you are below the ramp leading to the school. The metal railings on your left stand above an old well ❺. Reach this by going ahead a pace and taking the steps down to it on your left. It is known as Garsiwn

OWAIN GLYNDWR, PRINCE OF WALES

This engraving is of Glyndwr's seal. Fiercely nationalistic and determined to gain independence from the English, he fought a guerrilla war against them for many years. The mystery surrounding his death fuels the legend that Glyndwr will once more come down from the hills to do battle for Wales.

In the late-14th century, Wales was a subject nation longing for freedom. Prophecies abounded of the great leader destined, like a new Arthur, to free Wales. A poem of Taliesin, the Welsh bard, popular in the late 13th century, specified that Owain would lead this glorious attack. To his auspicious name were added the prophecies and visions of the descendants of the druids.

A descendant of the royal lines of Powys, Gwynedd and Deheubarth (Dyfed), Owain may have been born in 1349. He became 'a worthy gentleman; exceedingly well-read', studying law at the Inns of Court, London, before becoming a soldier. He served King Richard II in Scotland and, perhaps, Ireland.

This was a time of great social discontent, which was to manifest itself in Wales as nationalism. The spark to light this dry tinder was provided by Reginald Grey, Lord of Ruthin, an influential landowner who had seized part of Glyndwr's lands. Owain chose to fight him in the lawcourts, only to hear his case dismissed with the comment: 'What care we for barefoot Welsh dogs?'

On 16th September 1400, Owain was proclaimed Prince of Wales by a few family and friends and the red dragon standard of Wales was raised. The princedom he aspired to was no more than a state of mind, but the oppressed Welsh turned to Glyndwr. A territorial claim became a national struggle.

On 18th September, Owain's army attacked Ruthin. The fighting spread and King Henry IV came to put it down. Peace was secured by offering pardons, except to Owain, whose lands were confiscated. The English then showed their contempt for the Welsh by deciding, early in 1401, that no Welsh person could hold official office, or marry an English man or woman. The Welsh were not allowed to live in England and were to pay for their rebellion. This provoked further insurrection, more fighting against the English and eventually Glyndwr held Wales, apart from a few castles.

Harlech fell to Owain early in 1404 and he made its castle his base. Now he felt secure enough to call a parliament at Machynlleth, a convenient route centre. Owain was crowned and took the four lions of Gwynedd as his new coat of arms.

The vigorous Prince Henry, the future Henry V, was winning back South Wales, however, and Owain's days were numbered. In 1409, Harlech fell. Glyndwr, if he still was alive, was now just a guerrilla leader on the run. Like King Arthur, his end is shrouded in mystery.

soldiers used to be garrisoned here. This area was noted for its weavers' cottages in the early 19th century, before the woollen industry became concentrated in Yorkshire.

AN ASSASSIN'S GAOL

The Royal House **K** is where Dafydd Gam was imprisoned between 1404 and 1412. A loyal servant of the English King Henry IV, Glyndwr's arch-enemy, he had attempted to assassinate the great Welsh patriot. Later, he was to fight alongside Henry V at the Battle of Agincourt. The house acquired its royal name when Charles I stayed in it during a visit in 1643.

The Clock **L** was built to celebrate the coming of age of Charles Stewart Vane-Tempest, Viscount Castlereagh, the eldest son of the fifth Marquis of

▲*The Tourist Information Centre is housed in the Owain Glyndwr Institute and is built on the spot where the Welsh hero held his first parliament.*

Londonderry. The laying of the foundation stone was delayed for nearly a year until 15th July 1874, the day before Charles' twenty-second birthday. The 78-foot (23.4-metre) high tower stands on the site of the old Town Hall, where the court case described in George Borrow's classic travel book *Wild Wales* was held in 1854.

The Parliament House **N** may not date from 1404, but it is certainly medieval. This is the spot upon which Owain Glyndwr chose to hold a parliament and to be crowned.

Well ('garsiwn' means 'garrison') and its name derives from the time when the future Henry VII stopped here with his army on his way from Pembroke to the Battle of Bosworth Field in August, 1485. Henry's troops used the well, as did the majority of the population living at the western end of Machynlleth until relatively recently.

Poplar Square merges into Garsiwn Square **J**, indicating that

POWYS

A walk around countryside that inspired a great Welsh radical

▲*There are superb views across the valley from Braich-Odnant. The largest species of perching bird in the world, the raven (below) has been viewed for centuries as a harbinger of death and a bird of ill-omen.*

Llanbrynmair lies at the foot of a 1,300-foot (410-metre) hill, Newydd Fynyddog, that provides some of the best views in Wales from its high plateau. The mountains of southern Snowdonia, including Cadair Idris and Aran Fawddwy, can be seen to the north, while Plynlimon lies to the south. Prehistoric man chose this spot to build stone circles. These may have been places where the shamans experienced visions. A modern visionary, Samuel Roberts, was born and lived just below them.

NONCONFORMIST HOTBED

Llanbrynmair ⒶA is a village that moved to its present position, on what was the turnpike road, in the early 19th century. The Wynnstay Arms Hotel served the road, which was soon followed by the coming of the railway. The original village had clustered around what is still the parish church at Llan, 2 miles (3.2 km) south along the B4518. Llanbrynmair means 'St Mary's sacred enclosure on the hill'. Its circular graveyard suggests an ancient holy site. Later, Llanbrynmair was to

- ☀ Llanbrynmair, Powys

- ⬛ Pathfinder 886 (SH 80/90), grid reference SH 899028

  miles 0 1 2 3 4 5 6 7 8 9 10 miles
  kms 0 1 2 3 4 5 6 7 8 9 10 11 12 13 14 15 kms

- ◔ Allow 3½ hours

- ▲ Strenuous, with a climb to 1,300 feet (396 metres). Walking shoes are recommended. The route is well waymarked

- P Car park beside the A470 opposite the Wynnstay Arms Hotel at the start

- T Tel. (0891) 910910 for buses from Machynlleth and Newtown

- ▦ Refreshments in Llanbrynmair (Wynnstay Arms Hotel or Yr Hen Efail Tea Rooms)

- WC In the car park

THE WALK

LLANBRYNMAIR – DIOSG

The walk begins at the Wynnstay Arms Hotel, Llanbrynmair, on the A470. There is a car park across the road and a bus stop.

1 Face the Wynnstay Arms Hotel and go right to the road junction in the centre of Llanbrynmair **A**. Turn right along the B4518 towards Staylittle. Reach Yr Hen Efail Tea Rooms and Craft Shop on your right.

2 Turn left up a track immediately after a garage on your left. After 120 yards (108 metres), turn right over a stile and bear left, as waymarked. Go ahead over another stile to enter a field at a corner. Walk with a hedge on your right, continue over a stile in a corner and go ahead to another stile.

3 Cross the stile to walk with a hedge now on your left. Go through a gap to the next field and veer right to reach a track near a farm building. Turn right along the track.

4 Follow the track as it bends left and climbs to bend left again. Leave the track when it bends right. Follow the waymarked right-of-way uphill.

5 Take the waymarked gate at the top and bear right. Cross a stile in the fence on your right, then bear left up the track again. Ignore a downhill fork on your right.

6 At the top of the track, bear left to a waymark post on the skyline. Veer right to the next waymark post and continue to cross a fence by the tiniest of stiles. Go ahead to the next post.

7 Continue over a stile in the fence ahead and veer slightly left across a field to a stile in the next fence. Cross this to see Cerrig Caerau stone circle **B**.

8 Return over the stile and notice another stone circle **C** on your right as you retrace your steps to the previous stile. Cross it and veer very slightly right across the plateau and down through heather and bilberries as waymarked, to a lower fence.

9 Turn right to descend with the fence on your left. Turn left over waymarked stile, then turn right to walk down the valley above the stream on your right. Diosg **D** is below you.

10 Ignore a stile in the fence ahead (giving access to Braich-Odnant farmhouse). Go left, as waymarked, with the fence on your right. Go through a gate to a track, cross a bridge and reach a lay-by alongside the A450. Turn right along this road, into Dol-fâch.

11 Turn left at the telephone box up a no-through road. Cross the railway carefully at a level crossing and pass Yr Hen Gapel **E** on your right. Continue to where the road forks and turn left over a waymarked stile beside a gate. Veer very slightly left along Glyndwr's Way **F** to a waymarked stile in the far corner of this field. Cross it and turn left to pass a building on your left.

12 Go ahead over a stile to the right of a gate. Veer very slightly right across a field and along a path through a copse to a stile in a fence on your right. Cross this and bear left to a waymarked stile in the fence just above a conifer plantation. Continue over it and beside the trees for 200 yards (180 metres), then bear right to a stile just below more forest. Turn right over it and descend diagonally to a stile beside a gate giving access to the railway **G**.

13 Cross the line with care and go ahead along a track through the farmyard at Coedcae back to the A470. Turn right along the road back to Llanbrynmair.

▲*The village of Llanbrynmair lies at the foot of Newydd Fynynddog. The ascent to the 1,300-foot (410-metre) high plateau (right) affords some of the finest views in Wales. The stones of Cerrig Caerau (below) have eroded over time to a circle of boulders.*

railway and the industrial revolution led to Llanbrynmair gaining the highest rate of emigration in Wales. This was a time of great social change and discontent, which Samuel Roberts commented on in his famous magazine *Y Cronicl*, founded in 1843.

STONE CIRCLES

The first of the prehistoric stone circles is Cerrig Caerau ❸. It has eight large stones and the five boulder-like stones, lying with their centres exactly on a circle, are in their original position. The remaining three, presumably fallen, long stones, lie with their ends on the same circle. About 150 yards (135 metres) to the north-north-east lies a second stone circle, Lled Croen-yr-ych ❹. Its name is significant, meaning the 'width of the ox's hide'. Research has shown that the interior of old stone circles can cause altered states of consciousness, related to a significant difference in such things as background radiation. We know from the old Welsh story *The Dream of Rhonabwy* in *The Mabinogion* that lying on an ox's hide was associated with visions, so perhaps this circle acquired its name because an ox's

▼*Rough, grass-covered mountain tracks lead back down the hillside towards the farmhouse at Diosg.*

become a hotbed of nonconformism, perhaps because a detachment of Oliver Cromwell's soldiers are known to have disbanded here.

The production of flannel was the local cottage industry, but this was destined to collapse very soon after its peak in 1840, when £8,000 worth of flannel was produced by 500 people in the area. The coming of the

hide was spread within it, for visionary purposes. There is also a local tale of an ox being tethered here and bellowing to its separated partner on another summit (possibly Moel Eiddew, to the north-west). Could this be a folk memory of a ley line? Both circles fit Thom's thesis

◀ *The farm of Diosg was Samuel Roberts' boyhood home and where his lifelong views on injustice were formed.*

for a megalithic yard. The first circle has a diameter of close to 70 feet (21 metres), while Lled Croen-yr-ych's diameter is about 80 feet (24 metres). Its stones are smaller and appear to number seven.

GLYNDWR'S WAY

Diosg **D** is the farm where Samuel Roberts lived in the 19th century. He succeeded his father as minister at Yr Hen Gapel **E**. The return route

▲ *Yr Hen Gapel, where Samuel Roberts succeeded his father as minister, was a radical stronghold in the 19th century.*

follows part of Glyndwr's Way **F**. This long distance path covers about 120 miles (192km) between Knighton and Welshpool, via Machynlleth — where Owain Glyndwr was crowned as the last native, independent Prince of Wales. Its route is being 'fine-tuned' in preparation for its designation as an official National Trail by the Countryside Council for Wales.

Samuel Roberts

A great nonconformist radical, pacifist and pioneer, Samuel Roberts used his pen as his chief weapon against all social injustice.

Yr Hen Gapel was built at Dol-fâch in 1739 to serve the local Independents or Congregationalists. The nonconformist chapels were the places where radical views were vented in the late 18th and early 19th centuries.

Here, at the chapel's house, was born Samuel Roberts, on 6th March, 1800. He was the son of John Roberts, the minister. Long before his death in 1885, S R, as he was known, had earned a reputation as a great nonconformist radical. Literature was the instrument by which he delivered his message. Educated at the Independents' College at Llanfyllin and ordained in 1826, he took over at Yr Hen Gapel upon the death of his father in 1834. S R's father had moved the family to Diosg in 1810, so Samuel Roberts was to gain first hand knowledge of the plight of the smallholder. His hatred of the wickedness of the landowners, including Sir W W Wynn, has been recorded for posterity in his novel, *Ffarmwr Careful Cilhaul Uchaf (Farmer Careful of Cilhaul Uchaf).*

Diosg means 'the place of stripping' and S R's family was stripped of its investments here. As they improved the farm, their rent was increased. Having invested £700 in the property, John Roberts had no choice but to pay up, despite falling prices for farm produce. No wonder that injustice became a dominant theme in S R's writings. He wrote moving poetry against slavery, was famous for his addresses on the acceptance of death, especially among the young, whom he buried in his chapel

graveyard, and was a strong pacifist.

Ironically, when he emigrated to the USA in 1857, hoping to found a Utopian community, he landed in the Civil War. All around him he saw the name of Christianity dishonoured. When he returned to Wales in 1868, a staggering £1,245 was accepted as a testimonial for him. He went to live with his brother in Conwy and resumed the editorship of *Y Cronicl* upon his brother's death in 1884. Gladstone had sent S R a bounty of £50 in 1882 in recognition of his work for postal reforms, which anticipated those of Sir Rowland Hill. A pioneer in many respects, he died in Conwy on 24th September, 1885.

▲ *The railway arrived in 1861 but, sadly, the village station is now closed and the trains no longer stop here.*

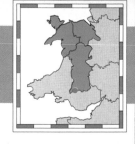

◀ *Legend surrounds Sgwd yr Eira on the River Hepste, where a path leads behind the cascading falls. This is also a favourite nesting place of the dipper (above).*

A fascinating adventure to some of Wales' most beautiful waterfalls

In this unique and beautiful corner of the Brecon Beacons National Park, several rivers drain from the moorland heights of Fforest Fawr to flow through wooded and rocky gorges where the forces of nature have created a remarkable series of waterfalls and cave systems.

The walk starts just above the entrance to Porth yr Ogof Cave ⓐ. Measuring 16 feet (5 metres) high and 57 feet (17 metres) wide, it is the largest cave entrance in Wales.

WHITE HORSE CAVE

There are no less than 14 different entrances, but these should only be used by agile and experienced cavers — the casual visitor should just walk a short distance into the main entrance. About 100 feet (30 metres) inside the cavern you may glimpse a calcite streak on the rock ahead of you which resembles a horse's head. At one time it used to

be known as White Horse Cave due to this natural feature.

Just a little further on the route, a path leads you along a river bed. Here you can see the original route of the River Mellte ⓑ before it took to its underground course. This often happens in limestone areas, and the resulting water channels are concealed from view until their roofs collapse and a series of caverns is transformed into a gorge.

After a while, you will come to a

rocky platform: this is where the River Mellte emerges from its underground journey about 300 yards (274 metres) from the main entrance of the cave. The beautiful pool in the river at this point is known as the Blue Pool ⓒ.

Shortly afterwards, you will catch a glimpse of the first waterfall (Sgwd Clun-gwyn ⓓ) along the route. Generally referred to as the 'Upper Fall', this is a spectacular site and a taste of what is to come.

▼ *The walk starts near the cave entrance to Porth yr Ogof, which is the largest in Wales.*

FACT FILE

✳ Near the village of Ystradfellte, about 5 miles (8 km) to the north-east of Glyn Neath off the A465

▭ Outdoor Leisure Map 11, grid reference SN 928124

miles 0 1 2 3 4 5 6 7 8 9 10 miles
kms 0 1 2 3 4 5 6 7 8 9 10 11 12 13 14 15 kms

◔ Allow 4 hours

▲ Not suitable for young children, or for dogs

Ⓟ At starting point

WC At the public car park

THE WALK

PORTH YR OGOF

The walk starts from the car park above the entrance to Porth yr Ogof Cave Ⓐ, which is situated about 1 mile (1.6 km) to the south of the little village of Ystradfellte.

1 To visit the entrance to the cave, go over a stile at the bottom of the car park and descend a steep and rocky path that leads down into the valley below. Turn left at the bottom and shortly you will see the wide entrance to Porth yr Ogof. Retrace your steps back to the car park.

2 Cross the road from the car park entrance and, by a footpath sign, go through a gate to follow a path that takes you along the old bed of the River Mellte Ⓑ. In due course you will come to a rocky platform overlooking the pool Ⓒ where the river reappears after its underground journey. Go back up to the path above to shortly descend to the bank of the river.

3 Continue along the path beside the river to reach a footbridge. Do not go across it but turn left and follow a waymarked route up the slope above. It will lead you to a point where you can look down on the first waterfall, the 'Upper Fall', which is called Sgwd Clun-gwyn Ⓓ.

4 Carry on along the path and in due course bear left at the next junction to follow the waymarked route. In case you have missed the first waymark, there should be another one further up the path. The path leads you up a side valley to reach a fence, which you follow to the right. From here you can enjoy views down into the Mellte Valley.

5 Continue on top path until you reach a junction with large signboard showing a path on the right to 'Lower Clun-gwyn Falls.' This brings you down to river level once more. Turn right and go up-river to reach the 'Middle Fall': Swgd Isaf Clun-gwyn Fall Ⓔ.

6 Retrace your steps and continue along the river bank, now following a broad path to reach the last fall on the Mellte, Sgwd y Pannwr Ⓕ.

7 From here the path crosses a rocky section to the left and then goes up a slope to reach a flat area where you can enjoy good views down the valley towards the Vale of Neath. Continue along the waymarked route and bear left to reach the top level path once more.

8 Turn right and listen for the sound of another waterfall. In due course you will be able to look through a gap in the trees and see Sgwd yr Eira Ⓖ in the valley below. If you decide to visit this fall, descend with care a long flight of steps that leads down on the right to about 200 feet (60 metres) below, and bear in mind that you will have to climb back up!

9 From the top of the steps go left over a stile to follow a path through a dark wood. When you emerge from the trees, turn right and head up a short slope, to turn left along a broad track.

10 On reaching a gate across the track, go over a stile and follow a fence in front of a farm house. Shortly you will join a lane that leads you back to the starting point at Porth yr Ogof Cave car park.

Further up-river you reach Sgwd Isaf Clun-gwyn waterfall Ⓔ. This is often called the 'Middle Fall' and is the widest of the waterfalls in this area. It is sometimes said to resemble a miniature Niagara Falls, with the water cascading over a curved platform of rock.

The last fall on River Mellte is

◀ Originating in the Fforest Fawr, the River Mellte winds its way through wooded and rocky gorges.

Sgwd y Pannwr Ⓕ. Also referred to as the 'Lower Clun-gwyn Fall', this is a smaller fall than the others but, split into several cascades, it can be just as beautiful.

Although less accessible than the others, the best-known waterfall in the area is undoubtedly the Sgwd yr Eira Ⓖ or 'Spout of Snow'. Its great attraction is that it is possible to follow a path behind the falling water, which is thrown clear of the ledge by an overhanging rock.

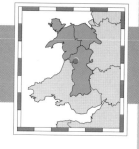

◀Near the Severn Flume, the river cascades dramatically over rocks. The marsh violet (inset) has adapted to life by the waterside, and produces its flowers in early summer.

3.3 on the Richter scale, was centred near here on 15 April 1984.

Hafren Forest was not planted until 1937. Before then, the car park was occupied by a farmhouse called Rhyd-y-Benwch.

WATER WORKS

The deep pool at the foot of the Cascades Ⓐ was used by shepherds to wash their sheep. The Severn Flume Ⓑ measures the river discharge of the Severn. It is at this point that you can extend the walk to the source, in a peat bog on

---

FACT FILE

✳	Hafren Forest
⌖	Pathfinder 928 (SN 88/98), grid reference SN 857869

miles 0　1　2　3　4　5　6　7　8　9　10 miles
kms 0　1　2　3　4　5　6　7　8　9　10　11　12　13　14　15 kms

◔	Allow 2 hours
▭	Mostly forest tracks. Narrow riverbank paths may be muddy. Walking boots recommended
P	Forestry Commission car park off a minor road in the Hafren Forest
WC	Toilets at the car park.

A walk through a mysterious forest beside Britain's longest river

Hafren Forest has a distinctive, almost brooding atmosphere. Although not native trees, the conifers that grow in the forest add much to its mood with their sombre magnificence.

Navigation is made easy on this walk by the frequent waymark posts that are provided by the Forestry Commission. If you get the taste for

adventure halfway around, simply extend this walk at Stage 6 by taking the white waymarked path ahead to reach the source of the River Severn, adding 3 miles (4.8 km) to this route's length.

In the forest itself, British Aerospace is testing aviation and satellite equipment. The site, in a disused quarry, has been chosen because it is remote and relatively free from electrical interference. The area does have other drawbacks, however, as it is known for its seismic activity. One of Britain's strongest earthquakes, measuring

▼After the flume, a footbridge crosses a quieter stretch of river and leads to a path through the forest.

THE WALK

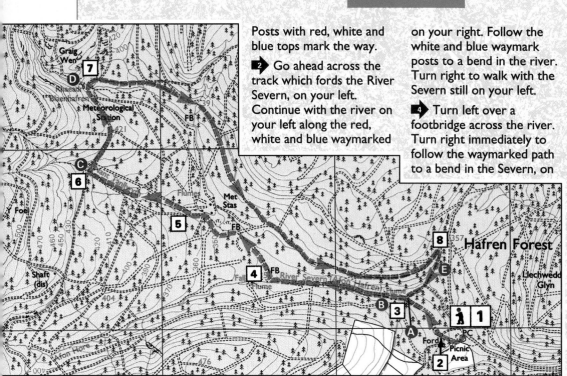

Posts with red, white and blue tops mark the way.

2 Go ahead across the track which fords the River Severn, on your left. Continue with the river on your left along the red, white and blue waymarked

on your right. Follow the white and blue waymark posts to a bend in the river. Turn right to walk with the Severn still on your left.

4 Turn left over a footbridge across the river. Turn right immediately to follow the waymarked path to a bend in the Severn, on

left along the signposted path to Blaenhafren, with the stream on your left. The waymark posts are still painted white and blue.

6 The white waymarked route **C** goes ahead when you reach a broad, firm track. This walk, though, turns right along it, waymarked by blue posts. Ignore a track coming from your right and admire the waterfall **D** on the left.

7 Keep to the broad track as it curves right back towards Rhyd-y-Benwch. Ignore all side tracks for 1½ miles (2.4 km) while you climb to a junction with a track marked with red posts on your right. Continue ahead a short distance, until you meet another track running downhill from left to right.

8 Turn right down the track and pass a red waymarking post on your right. Ignore a track through the trees **E** on your left. Go ahead to a junction with your outward path at the picnic site. Turn left to follow the River Severn on your right, back towards the car park and the start of the walk.

HAFREN FOREST

The walk begins at the Forestry Commission car park beside the minor road that goes through the Hafren Forest south of the B4518 at Staylittle.

1 Start from the information board in the car park. Follow the signposted Cascades Trail down through young Norwegian spruce trees.

path, which starts as a boardwalk.

3 The red waymarks signify the short Cascades Trail, which goes right into the forest at a picnic place near the Cascades **A**. The walk continues along the white and blue waymarked path above the River Severn on your left. Pass a flume (a ravine with a stream) **B** and ignore a track with blue waymarks

your right. Bear left to take the waymarked path through the forest. Avoid the inviting, wide forest rides. Follow the white and blue waymark posts along a narrow path through the trees. A tributary of the Severn (Nant Tanllwyth) is on your right. Ignore the first footbridge across it.

5 Cross the second footbridge over Nant Tanllwyth on your right. Go

Plynlimon at a height of over 2,000 feet (600 metres), by following the white waymarked route **C**. Rhaeadr Blaenhafren **D** is a distinctive, fan-shaped waterfall.

RIVER OF LEGEND

The English name Severn is a corruption of the Welsh Hafren, which is derived from Habren (Sabrina in English). She was the daughter of Locrinus, the eldest son of Brutus (who, according to legend, led the Trojans to Albion and renamed it Britain) and his mistress, Estrildis. Locrinus' wife Gwendolen (the daughter of the ruler of Cornwall) killed her errant husband and threw his mistress and daughter into the

river that now bears Sabrina's name.

At a length of 220 miles (352km), the River Severn is the longest river in Britain. Returning to the river-bank, the track passes Norwegian spruce (Christmas trees) on your right and Sitka spruce on your left **E**. The timber is made into paper pulp, chipboard and fence posts.

In the conifer plantations, look out for the rose-red male crossbill and his greener mate. They feed on the seeds of cones borne by the mature trees. The riverbank near the start of the walk is carpeted with mosses, including sphagnum. Marsh violets can be seen in the summer, when heather and gorse also add colour.

▼*The end of the walk leads along a broad track lined with wild flowers, silhouetted against dark conifers.*

ACROSS THE DESERT

▲ *The route passes through some fine, remote hill country and follows several rivers and streams. The buzzard (left) can often be seen circling lazily, high overhead, calling with a soft* 'mew'.

A drovers' route through the bare and isolated hills of mid-Wales

This walk through a quiet corner of Powys includes some of the finest scenery in the county. It starts at the remote hamlet of Abergwesyn **Ⓐ**, once a key stop for drovers as they moved livestock from west of here to the English borders.

Lichen-covered sessile oaks survive on the steepest hillsides and in deep dells around Abergwesyn, a remnant of the thick forest that once covered almost all of Wales. These woods, with their floor of mossy boulders, ferns and bracken, are enchanting all year round.

Much of the original oak forest was thinned by medieval charcoal burners, then finally cleared in the 18th century to rid the area of cover for the two major menaces that drovers encountered — wolves and brigands. The first attacked sick or weak members of the herds; the second sought the cash being carried back to local farmers by drovers returning from the English markets. These twin evils were seen as such a threat to the commerce of the region that the land was stripped bare and was thenceforth known as 'the desert of Wales'.

The bleak but majestic valley that runs between Abergwesyn and Mynydd Trawsnant is an excellent example of surviving Welsh desert. The route follows close to the bottom of the valley and has been cut into the hillside in some sections to make the going easier.

This narrow track suited the drovers of hogs, and its Welsh name means 'the pig's way'. Fattened hogs moved slowly, so their drovers took advantage of short-cuts too narrow for sheep or cattle. The animals had to be muzzled when driven, to curb their natural instinct to stop and root for food. Their feet were shod with leather booties designed to protect their tender trotters.

In the days of the drovers, Llyn Brianne **Ⓑ** did not exist. However, the tarmac road on this side follows a wide main droving route along the 'false crest' of the hills. The crest sheltered the animals from harsh weather on the exposed heights above, but still allowed them to be seen and heard by the farmers below. In dry seasons, when the water level of Llyn Brianne drops, you can sometimes see the sunken farms, road and chapel that were lost to this enormous reservoir.

BRITAIN'S TALLEST DAM

The huge dam at Llyn Brianne, rising to a height of 300 feet (91m) above the level of the original river, is the tallest in Britain. It was designed to power the turbines of a South Walian industrial revival that never came. Today, the waters of the lake are cold, deep and unable to support fish due to an excess of acid rain. Further casualties of the

---

FACT FILE

✳ Abergwesyn, 4 miles (6.4km) north-west of Llanwrtyd Wells

▭▤ Pathfinders 991 (SN 85/95) and 1014 (SN 84/94), grid reference SN 853525

miles 0 1 2 3 4 5 6 7 8 9 10 miles
kms 0 1 2 3 4 5 6 7 8 9 10 11 12 13 14 15 kms

◔ Allow 3 to 4 hours

◣ Some strenuous hill walking in isolated and difficult terrain. Walking boots and weatherproof clothing are essential. The lack of landmarks in some sections means that a compass should be used

Ⓣ BR service to Llanwrtyd Wells, 4 miles (6.4km) from the start, and a very infrequent bus service to Abergwesyn

🍴 Grouse Inn in Abergwesyn (closed when farm is very busy); several pubs and hotels off the route in Llanwrtyd Wells

---

scheme were the chasms and head-waters of the Towy, once one of the finest salmon rivers in South Wales. Few salmon now bother to fight their way upstream to the spawning pools below the dam. Naturalists and anglers alike have cursed Llyn Brianne since its construction in the 1960s, but it has a powerful presence and is an unforgettable sight.

The finest views come on the return leg of the walk, on the path up to the high ground of Cefn Blaencwmhenog and Cefn Uchaf **C**, more than 1,600 feet (490m) above sea-level. To the west is a grand view of the mountains which Daniel Defoe once described as 'impassable', while the Brecon Beacons and Carmarthen Fans rise to the south. As you descend towards Abergwesyn, you can see the dramatic cliffs of Esgair Irfon, which tower over the pass and the modern road into the village from the north.

This road was built along the course of the same drovers' route encountered on the banks of Llyn Brianne. It has gone the long way around the mountain of Cefn Coch, which means the 'red hill' in Welsh but is now blue-green with forestry conifers. There is one final view of oak trees just before you join a road beside a winding river, and follow it back to Abergwesyn.

THE WALK

ABERGWESYN – LLYN BRIANNE

The walk starts by the old church, now a house, at the south-west of Abergwesyn **A**.

▶ **1** Cross the river, then turn right up the footpath along its bank, then bears left around a farm. Go uphill through oak trees until you reach a wide track. Keep right and follow the track for 100 yards (90m). Bear left by hazel bushes onto a grass track down to Llwynderw, a large Georgian house, formerly a hotel.

▶ **2** Pass the hotel on your left. Just before the drive, turn right on a clear track through pasture to a stream, Nant Rhyd-goch.

▶ **3** Cross the stream at the ford and follow the path uphill to a fork. Bear left towards the valley floor.

▶ **4** Cross another stream, Nant y Craf. Follow the path ahead along the valley, rising slightly then dropping

to go alongside the Nant Gwrach, just before it empties into Llyn Brianne **B**, to a road.

▶ **5** Turn left and follow this road as it winds uphill for a view of Llyn Brianne, then retrace your steps back to where the footpath turns uphill to the right.

▶ **6** Climb the path up Cefn Blaencwmhenog to the cairn **C** and continue across Nant Sarn to the forestry. The path to the cairn can be very indistinct and a compass may be required.

▶ **7** Go through a gate and follow the path east for about 400 yards (360m).

Fork north-west on a wider track which eventually leads out of the wood.

▶ **8** Turn left and head downhill, following the line of forestry and the scrub down to the valley floor. There has been much replanting here so the public right of way may be unclear.

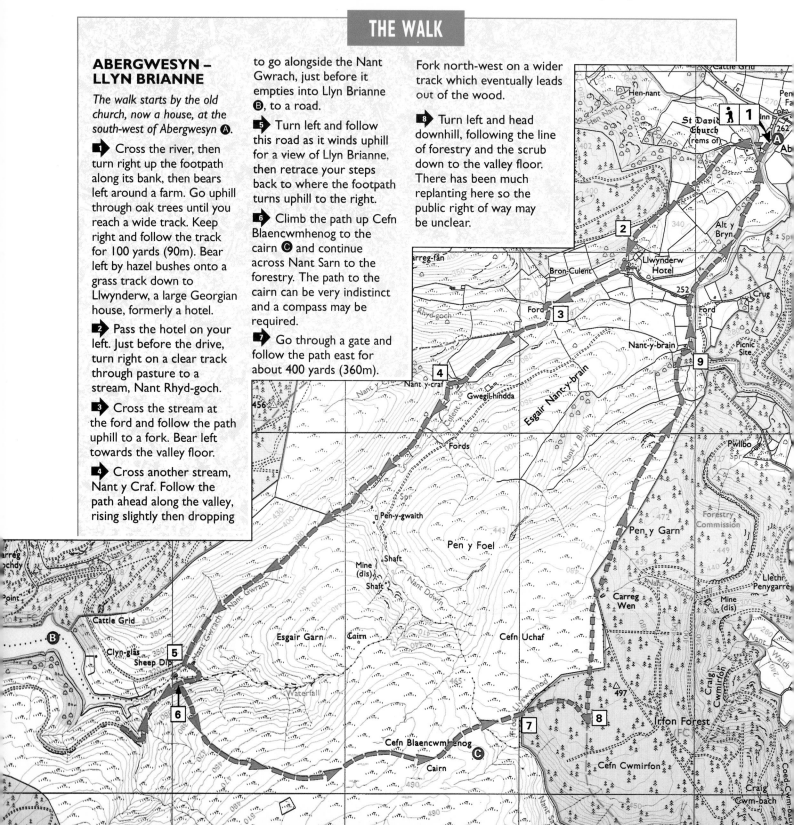

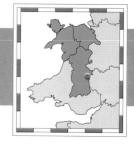

◀*New Radnor, which at one time was the county town of Radnorshire, is approached down leafy lanes. The redstart (inset) is a summer visitor and nests in the valley in tree holes.*

A ramble through the heart of the old county of Radnorshire

The ancient towns of New and Old Radnor, which today are little more than villages, are on opposing flanks of a tranquil valley. Old Radnor is in the shadow of St Stephen's Church **A**, 840 feet (254m) above sea-level. The breathtakingly beautiful interior of the church features a medieval oak wagon roof enriched with heavily carved bosses, while an exquisite 15th-century screen runs across its entire width. The organ case is the oldest in Britain, but perhaps the greatest treasure is the stone font, over 1,200 years old and probably put to sacred use in pre-Christian times.

The route heads gently down, up and then down again, between hedgerows which yield an abundant harvest of blackberries, rosehips and elderberries and sometimes meet overhead to create a green corridor.

Lanes lead you to New Radnor, and one of the finest examples of a Victorian memorial **B** in the country. Towering nearly 80 feet (24m) high, it commemorates the politician Sir George Cornewall Lewis.

Above the shaded graveyard of Victorian St Mary's Church **C** are the grassy mounds of New Radnor Castle **D**, overlooking what was a main route into central Wales. Harold, last Saxon King of England, is credited with building the once sizeable motte and bailey as an outpost against the understandably hostile Welsh. In 1401, Owain Glyndwr, the self-proclaimed Prince of Wales who led the last major rebellion against the English, ransacked the town. The castle's 60-strong garrison were all killed, and the castle ceased to be effective.

Narrow, twisting lanes lead back to Old Radnor. In a field by the roadside, four massive standing stones **E** supposedly mark the burial sites of four warrior kings. Legend has it that they wait for the peal of St Stephen's bell, the signal for them to lumber down to nearby Lake Hindwell for a cooling drink.

FACT FILE

- Old Radnor, 12 miles (19.2km) east of Llandrindod Wells, off the A44

- Pathfinders 971 (SO 26/36) and 993 (SO 25/35), grid reference SO 250590

  | miles 0 | 1 | 2 | 3 | 4 | 5 | 6 | 7 | 8 | 9 | 10 miles |
  | kms 0 1 2 3 4 5 6 7 8 9 10 11 12 13 14 15 kms |

- Allow 3½ hours

- Easy walking on mostly level woodland paths and quiet country lanes

- **P** Car park at the start

- Pubs in Old and New Radnor

- Restaurants and a coffee shop in New Radnor

- **I** Tourist Information at Presteigne, Tel. (01544) 260193

THE WALK

OLD RADNOR – NEW RADNOR

The walk begins from the car park opposite St Stephen's Church Ⓐ in Old Radnor.

1 Cross the road into St Stephen's churchyard. Leave by the side gate and turn right, then left down a narrow lane. At a farm, bend left, then right, following the track around the buildings and out past the farmhouse. Follow the track down, then cross two fields, keeping close to the hedge. Go through a gate to cross the old railway line and join a narrow path, passing houses on your left.

2 Turn right along the lane, and continue to the triangle at the crossroads by a chapel. Bear to the right of the triangle and go straight across onto a track. At a gate, bear right along a corridor of mature hedgerows. Go over a crossroads and straight on to join a forestry track down through pine woods and out onto a main road.

3 Turn left, then soon right towards New Radnor. Pass to the left of a Victorian memorial Ⓑ and turn left into Rectory Lane. Continue ahead across the High Street and up some steps, turning left past the war memorial to St Mary's Church Ⓒ. Follow the path to the right of the church, through a kissing-gate. Bear left uphill to the mound of New Radnor Castle Ⓓ. From here, retrace your steps to the war memorial and continue straight on along the High Street.

4 At a junction, bear left and follow the road for approximately 2 miles (3.2km), towards Kinnerton. At a crossroads at the bottom of the hill, turn right and walk down the narrow Crossfield Lane. At a T-junction, turn right and continue past the four standing stones Ⓔ to the A44.

5 Cross with care, and continue along a track beside the cottage slightly to your left. Where the track bends left, go straight on through a gate into a field. Head uphill and across a stile in the top left-hand corner, onto a road. Turn right to return to the car park.

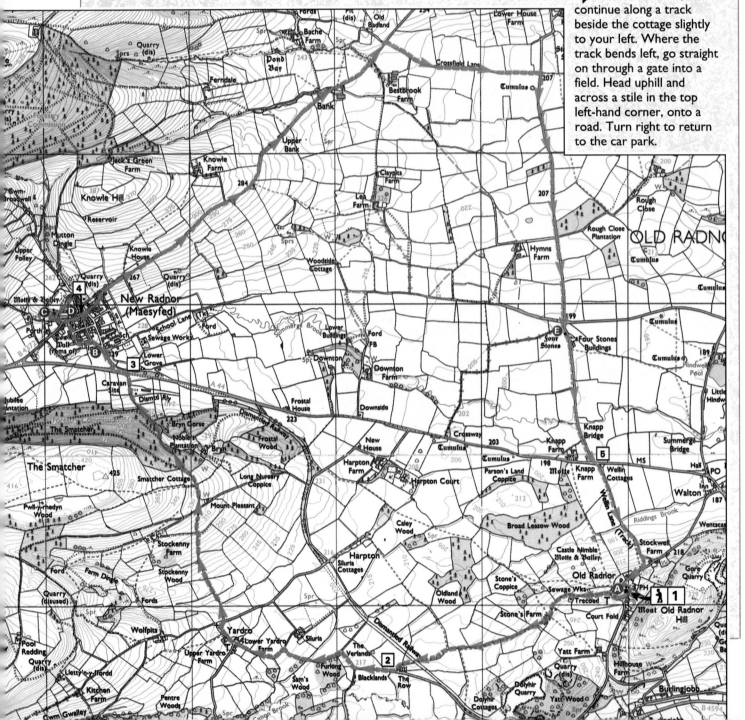

ON THE BEACONS

A magnificent walk to one of the high points of the Brecon Beacons

▲*Looking back along the narrow ridge of Bwlch y Ddwyallt to the hill on the northern leg of the route. The Bewick's swan (inset) visits the reservoir in winter; it spends the summer in Siberia.*

The Brecon Beacons National Park is fine, if strenuous, country, with dramatic scenery and sweeping views. This walk begins by crossing a deep gully, down which a stream tumbles in a series of waterfalls ❶ between rock walls overhung with ferns. It then follows an unfenced moorland road below a hillside, where ponies munch alongside the sheep.

As the road approaches a cattle grid, a broad level track sweeps on to the left. This is the track bed of the Brecon and Merthyr Tydfil Junction Railway, which somehow found a way through the hills. A section to the south is now used by the Brecon Mountain Railway.

The walk leaves the road for a forest track across a small stream, a popular spot with grey wagtails. This is a typically dense conifer plantation, but the track edge is enlivened by foxgloves and patches of bright, orange-red sandstone.

The woodland gradually gives way to more open ground with birch trees, patches of gorse and little streams running in deep gullies. The track follows the edge of the wood, then crosses a small stream and runs at a gentle angle uphill.

At first, the tower at Upper Neuadd Reservoir ❷ appears, like a church among the trees, then the whole reservoir gradually comes into sight, with the great sweeping bulk of the Beacons ahead. This is an old track, crossing the Beacons at a saddle between two hills.

The sandstone underfoot appears as flat plates. The hills rise, rounded and smooth, from the south, to end in near vertical escarpments fringed with crags. Looking back, you can see down the length of the valley to the hills beyond.

This is a very open track, but there is no lack of company. The bleating of sheep echoes round the valley, joined by the exquisite song of hovering skylarks and the sharp 'chack, chack', alternating with bursts of song, of the wheatears.

The path almost reaches the saddle, then turns back on itself, appearing as a vivid scar on the land as it heads, more steeply, to the top of the hill ❸, a summit of shattered stone and rock. The earth suddenly falls away in a steep escarpment and you look into the great bowl of a natural amphitheatre. The highest point of the Beacons is far to the left; here, a plateau extends for over a mile (1.6km) to the promontory on the far side of the bowl.

PEATY PLATEAU

The top is an area of peat and thin soil, with cotton grass flecking the green. There has been a good deal of erosion, leaving mushroom-like hummocks, fringed with a curtain of white wool where sheep have rubbed up against them. Near the cliff edge, the soil has disappeared, leaving the rock exposed in slabs.

Looking into the bowl, you can see the valley sides slowly steepen until they reach the escarpment, where a ring of small crags mimics contour lines on a map. Streams snake down from the hills into the lusher grassland of the Usk Valley.

The path along the lip of the plateau becomes narrower and stonier as it runs along a ridge

---

FACT FILE

❋ Blaen-y-glyn, 7½ miles (12km) south of Brecon, on the Merthyr Tydfil to Talybont-on-Usk road

▦ Outdoor Leisure 11 Brecon Beacons, grid reference SO 056175

miles 0 1 2 3 4 5 6 7 8 9 10 miles
kms 0 1 2 3 4 5 6 7 8 9 10 11 12 13 14 15 kms

◷ Allow 4 hours

▲ A strenuous and remote hill walk, with one steep descent, mostly on open moorland. Walking boots and weatherproof clothing essential

P Forestry Commission car park at start

🍴 None on route

THE WALK

BRECON BEACONS

Begin at the Forestry Commission car park at Blaen-y-glyn on the back road between Merthyr Tydfil and Talybont-on-Usk.

1 Leave the car park by the approach road, crossing the gully by the waterfalls **A**, and turn right at the road.

2 Beyond the cattle grid, turn right onto the gravel forestry road. The track divides: follow it round to the right.

3 Where the gravel track swings sharply right and begins to climb, go ahead through the wooden gate.

4 At the road turn right, then right again up the track signposted to Brecon via Bwlch ar y Fan.

5 At the end of the woodland, cross the stile on the left and continue on the path across the stream. Follow the path bearing right uphill above the reservoir **B**.

6 Just before reaching the top of the pass, turn back sharp right to take the narrow path, heading uphill.

7 At the top of the hill **C** follow the path around the rim of the plateau.

8 The path rises to a narrow ridge **D**. As it dips, turn back to the right to take the path following the opposite side of the ridge.

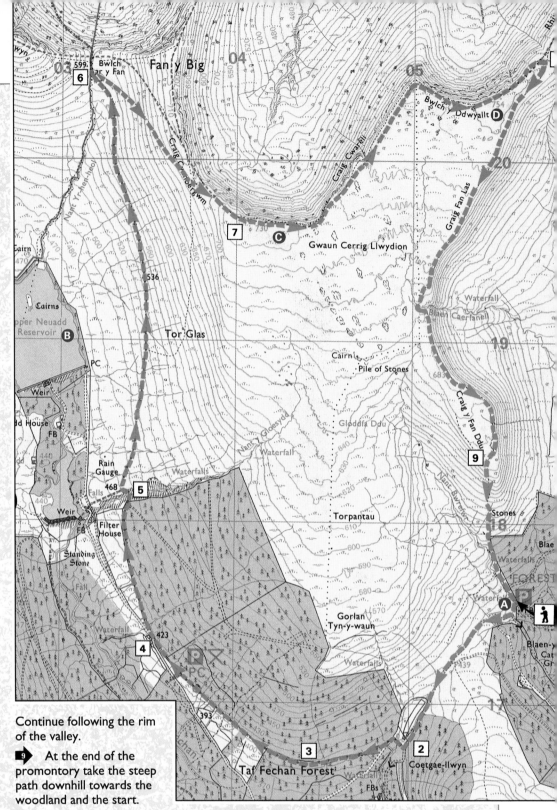

Continue following the rim of the valley.

9 At the end of the promontory take the steep path downhill towards the woodland and the start.

poking out towards the north. At the end of the ridge **D**, a whole new view opens up to the right into another valley. A stream tumbles down from the plateau and runs off to dark patches of woodland and a succession of rounded hills, receding into the distance.

The path is now very narrow,

◀ *A view from the track down to Upper Neuadd Reservoir and its dam.*

running above the top of steep slopes. The plateau is drained by a stream that falls down a series of rock ledges, like a stone staircase. At the end you descend first on a gentle, grass slope, then a steep, eroded and shaly path.

The final stage runs by the rocky gully first seen at the beginning of the walk. Here there is a whole series of high falls, dropping from ledges overhung by trees.

Country lanes and airy moorland tracks near a Norman castle

▲*Tretower Castle's tower and keep were part of the Norman defences of the Usk Valley. The wheatear (above left) can be seen and heard on high ground from early spring through the summer.*

The little village of Tretower has an interesting mix of buildings. The most impressive of them is Tretower Court **A** (see box on page 116), where this walk begins. In addition, there is a rather grand farmhouse, the windows of which have hexagonal panes, along with a selection of houses in the dark, reddish-brown local stone, though some of these have been given a smooth stucco finish.

As the route leaves Tretower Court, the tower of Tretower's Norman castle rears up from the fields to the left. At the end of a short section of road is a small chapel, with an inscription stating that it was erected by Zoar in 1844. It has since been converted into an unusual but handsome dwelling.

The walk leaves the road for a broad farm track across the fields that crowd the broad, flat, valley floor. The hills rising up on every side seem to consist of a series of ledges, as the smooth curve is broken by escarpments.

A concrete slab bridge takes you across a little river, the Rhiangoll, to a path beside a tall hedge. Here, the fields are a mixture of crops and pasture, and this part of the walk is very easy going, with ever-changing views down the valleys that open out to either side.

FORT AND FARMS

You cross a little flagstone bridge and continue down a green lane between ferny banks that rise above head height to a trio of farms — Lower, Middle and Upper Gaer. There is an interesting array of farm buildings, some of them converted for housing, while a barn at Middle Gaer has unusual pointed arches and signs of a former chimney, suggesting it was once a house.

The road leads past the farm of Pen-y-gaer, which is enclosed by a grassy bank visible on both sides of the road. This square earthwork was part of a small Roman fort **B**. The

FACT FILE

✳ Tretower, 8½ miles (13.6km) south-east of Brecon, on the A479

▭ Pathfinder 1062 (SO 02/12), or Outdoor Leisure Map 13, grid reference SO 186211

miles 0 1 2 3 4 5 6 7 8 9 10 miles
kms 0 1 2 3 4 5 6 7 8 9 10 11 12 13 14 15 kms

◷ Allow 4 to 5 hours

◠ Relatively easy going underfoot most of the way, but over 1,000 feet (305m) between lowest and highest points of walk. Some short, steep ascents and descents. Should not be attempted during wet weather, when some sections are very muddy

ℙ Opposite Tretower Court at the start

▦ Pub at Cwmdu

⌶ Tretower Court is open daily; Apr-Oct 9.30am-6pm, Nov-Mar 9.30am-4pm. Tel. (01874) 730279 for further details

artificial platform is most clearly seen beyond the farmhouse.

This short section of road walking ends at the next junction, where a path leads uphill through an avenue of gnarled trees; there are some impressive beech trees, but the grandest are the massive oaks, with their short sturdy trunks and wide-spreading branches.

The going gets rougher, with stone pushing up through the soil.

The path is clearly an old route; there are remains of stone walls on the banks. It is easier to walk on the grass at the side of the track than on the gully-like path. This has the added advantage of giving fine

THE WALK

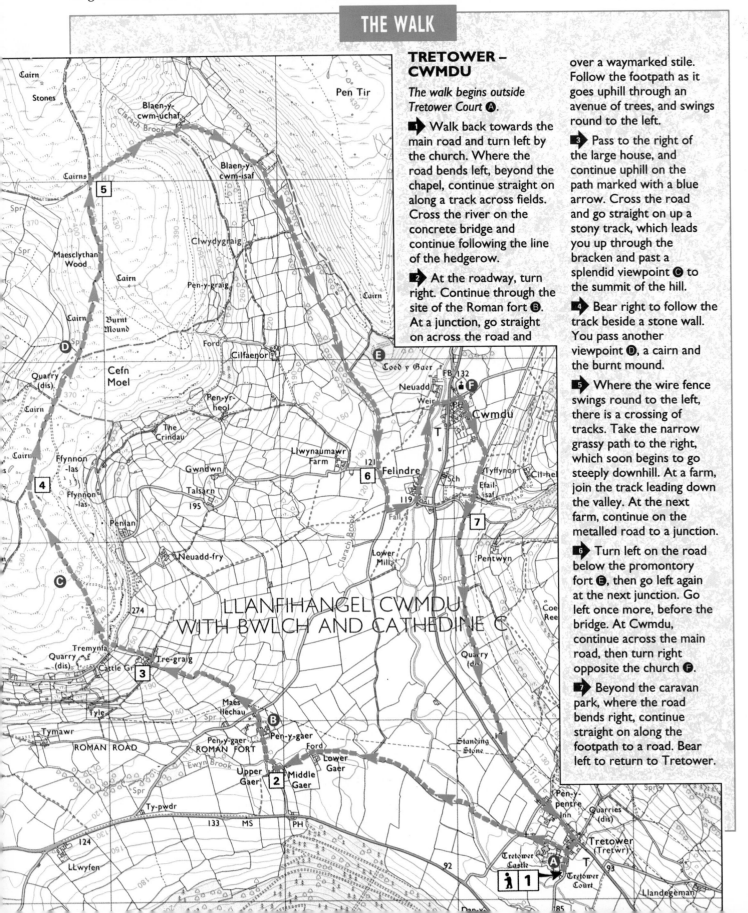

TRETOWER – CWMDU

The walk begins outside Tretower Court **A**.

1 Walk back towards the main road and turn left by the church. Where the road bends left, beyond the chapel, continue straight on along a track across fields. Cross the river on the concrete bridge and continue following the line of the hedgerow.

2 At the roadway, turn right. Continue through the site of the Roman fort **B**. At a junction, go straight on across the road and over a waymarked stile. Follow the footpath as it goes uphill through an avenue of trees, and swings round to the left.

3 Pass to the right of the large house, and continue uphill on the path marked with a blue arrow. Cross the road and go straight on up a stony track, which leads you up through the bracken and past a splendid viewpoint **C** to the summit of the hill.

4 Bear right to follow the track beside a stone wall. You pass another viewpoint **D**, a cairn and the burnt mound.

5 Where the wire fence swings round to the left, there is a crossing of tracks. Take the narrow grassy path to the right, which soon begins to go steeply downhill. At a farm, join the track leading down the valley. At the next farm, continue on the metalled road to a junction.

6 Turn left on the road below the promontory fort **E**, then go left again at the next junction. Go left once more, before the bridge. At Cwmdu, continue across the main road, then turn right opposite the church **F**.

7 Beyond the caravan park, where the road bends right, continue straight on along the footpath to a road. Bear left to return to Tretower.

▶*The meadows by the rivers provide good grazing for cattle, a scarce commodity in the surrounding hills.*

views across to the hills on the left.

You meet a roadway by a group of imposing stone houses. The hillside steepens and a small stream burbles through the rocks to one side of the path, which is still overshadowed by small trees. A track, with great slabs of sandstone underfoot, leads up to a point ⓒ where a splendid panorama opens out.

SUGAR LOAF

To the east is the shapely outline of the Sugar Loaf mountain, above Abergavenny, and the rounded hump of the Blorenge, lying further south on the opposite side of the Usk Valley. From here, the wooded hill above Tretower appears as an isolated hump, and the view stretches over it to the next valley.

The broad track climbs steadily to the ridge of Cefn Moel, at a height of nearly 1,200 feet (366m) above sea level. On the top, the bracken is broken by patches of gorse and rough grass, and a dry-stone wall snakes along the crest of the ridge.

The hills are far from deserted; wild ponies graze among the sheep, and the air is loud with birdsong — from the harsh chatter of the stonechat and the wheatear to the tuneful trill of the skylark and the distant mew of a hunting buzzard.

There are signs of man's presence in the remains of small quarries, a cairn and, on the horizon, the ruler-straight edge of a forestry plantation. At a break in the high stone wall, there is a view ⓓ over to the other side of the ridge. Down below is Llangorse Lake, busy with sailing boats in summer, and beyond that the great mass of the Brecon Beacons. Here, at the top of the hill, the few trees are bent almost horizontal by the prevailing winds.

BURNT MOUND

Just beyond the viewpoint is a rounded grassy hill with a small cairn of stones, and nearby is a crescent-shaped, overgrown mound of stones. In the Iron Age, water for cooking was heated by throwing in hot stones from a fire. As they broke they were removed and piled up to create a Burnt Mound, like this one.

You descend gently, then turn off to the right on a narrow, grassy path through the bracken, which heads steeply down into a deep valley, its sides studded with scrubby trees. A stream, the Clarach Brook, tumbles down to a small farmhouse sitting at the head of the valley, surrounded by a noisy clutter of sheep, goats, dogs and chickens. With its whitewashed walls and grey slate roof, it is the epitome of a hill farm.

The route continues along the farm track beside the stream to a second, larger farmhouse, with neat dormer windows. Beyond it, you join a country lane that runs

◀*The lime-washed farm building at Pen-y-gaer ('gaer' means 'castle') is built on the site of a Roman fort. As the route climbs along Cefn Moel, there are splendid views east (above) across the valley to the distant wooded slopes.*

◄Cwmdu's church, set on a mound to the north of the village, commands the entrance to the Rhiangoll Valley. Back in Tretower, a chapel (below), built in 1844, is now an unusual family home.

between high beech hedges. In this enclosed world, the banks on either side are bright with flowers, whose heavy scent seems to be trapped in the deep lane.

COED Y GAER

As the road runs into a little wood, it begins to drop quite steeply, with tall ferns on one side and dense, coppiced woodland on the other. To the left is a steep hillside, covered with trees. The route runs round this hill, which is revealed as a long promontory. Its steep sides made it an ideal natural defensive position, and Iron Age settlers built a rampart and ditch across its neck to create a small fort, Coed y Gaer **E**.

An old two-arched stone bridge crosses the river, which tumbles over a low weir at the edge of Cwmdu. A mill once stood at the site. The houses are a mixture of old and new, some whitewashed, some left as dull, brownish-red sandstone.

The road crosses a single-arched bridge to come to the village pub, opposite which, on a slight rise, stands the Parish Church of Michael the Archangel **F**.

The church's most prominent feature is its sturdy crenellated tower, but there is an interesting detail on the buttress between the two porches. An ancient gravestone has been let into the wall and its inscription reads 'Here lies Catloc the son of Teyrnoc' in Celtic script. It was brought here by the Reverend T Lewis in the last century.

OLD ROAD

The final part of the route runs past a large but well-screened caravan park, then continues along a footpath, an old road between Cwmdu and Tretower. Once again, grand old oak trees line and overshadow the route. In several places the path is a narrow, green corridor, and at one point plunges into a little rocky gully. It runs down to the main road that leads back into Tretower.

Tretower Castle and Tretower Court

Tretower Castle is a typical Norman fortress, built by Roger Picard as part of the defences of the Usk Valley. The tall tower within its shell keep looks as if it would have been impregnable in the years before gunpowder and the cannon changed the art of war, but it was captured by Llewellyn the Last in 1260 and later regained by the Picards.

In more peaceful times, the castle was abandoned for the fortified house of Tretower Court. From the outside, it still has a somewhat forbidding appearance, with its high stone walls and an

The well preserved gatehouse of Tretower Court, built in 1480, has a rather gaunt appearance, which belies the charmingly domestic atmosphere of the interior.

entrance guarded by a gatehouse. Ducts above the main gate were installed so that molten lead could be poured on any attackers. Inside, however, the whole appearance and atmosphere of the house alters, with an airy courtyard surrounded by a wooden gallery.

The house was begun in the 14th century, but the Vaughan family, who were its owners for many generations, introduced alterations in the 15th century. The medieval pattern, however, was preserved, and the spacious, oak-timbered rooms give an excellent idea of how comfortable life could be for the rich at the end of the Middle Ages. Notable among the owners of this splendid house was the 17th-century metaphysical poet, Henry Vaughan.

Exploring moorland and forestry beyond an important abbey

The beautiful Clywedog Valley in the forested hills of Powys shelters what is left of the largest ecclesiastical building in Wales, an abbey that fell into ruin following the Dissolution of the Monasteries. The remaining masonry, shrouded in the trees of a secluded meadow on the banks of the Clywedog Brook, is still an impressive sight.

VICTORIAN CHURCH

St Mary's, the parish church of Abbeycwmhir, the village that grew up around the monastic foundation, is the starting point for this walk around the area. Built in 1865-66 in the Early English style, it has a tower and spire that loom 75 feet (23m) above the entrance porch.

The chancel is divided from the nave by a moulded arch supported on columns of Peterhead granite. An ancient coffin lid, set into the wall, is

FACT FILE

⁂ Abbeycwmhir, 6 miles (9.6km) north of Llandrindod Wells, off the A483

▱ Pathfinders 949 (SO 07/17) and 970 (SO 06/16), grid reference SO 054712

miles 0 1 2 3 4 5 6 7 8 9 10 miles
kms 0 1 2 3 4 5 6 7 8 9 10 11 12 13 14 15 kms

◔ Allow 3 hours

▲ An energetic and challenging walk on sometimes ill-defined field paths and along forestry roads and tracks. One steep ascent. Some very boggy ground along the banks of the stream and in other areas. Walking boots are recommended

P Outside the church at the start

▦ The Happy Union Inn, Abbeycwmhir

I Tourist Information at Llandrindod Wells, Tel. (01597) 822600

▲*After climbing gently on a zigzag path, you can enjoy a fine view back over the fields through which you have come. The giant puffball (inset), which is edible, can occur in these fields.*

believed to be that of Mabli, a former abbot of Abbey Cwmhir.

The church's most memorable possession is a painting, *The Agony in the Garden*, hanging on the north wall of the nave. Left lying in the rubble when an earlier church was demolished, it was eventually rescued and put on display in the new church. However, it was so blackened that no-one could make out the subject, and it was hung upside-down for 25 years. When cleaned in 1892, it was revealed as an immensely powerful image, with Christ's glowing face lighting up His blue and white robes.

Not far away are the ruins of Abbey Cwmhir Ⓐ. Built in 1176, the abbey was the second Cistercian foundation in Wales, and designed on a scale far beyond the needs of its intended 60 resident monks. The abbey church had an ornately

Nature Walk

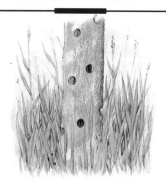

TREE GUARDS are put around young conifer trees to protect them from the attentions of grazing forest animals.

FIRE TOWERS, usually built on a high vantage point, allow wardens to keep a look-out for the forest's worst enemy.

SWING GATES are built to allow badgers to follow their regular paths through the line of new fencing.

BAT BOXES, fixed to the sides of tree trunks, encourage bats to roost; they enter through a slot in the bottom.

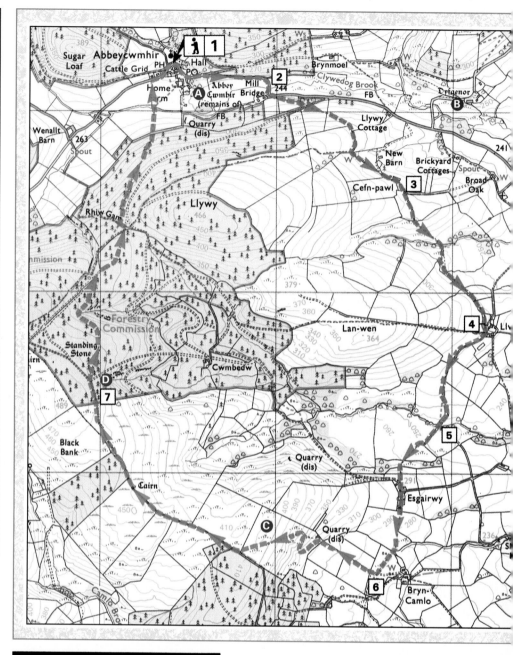

carved arcade of 14 bays on either side of the nave, the length of which, 242 feet (74m), was exceeded only by two or three cathedrals.

The abbey was caught up in the turbulent history of the Welsh borders, and the chancel was never completed. The abbey was never totally restored after being sacked and burnt by the Welsh rebel Owain Glyndwr in 1402. At the Dissolution, only three monks remained.

In the Civil War, it became a Royalist fortress, and was stormed and devastated by Roundheads in

◀ *This fine, geometrical tracery window in St Mary's Church, Abbeycwmhir has some richly coloured Victorian glass.*

THE WALK

ABBEYCWMHIR

The walk begins at the church, opposite The Happy Union Inn, in Abbeycwmhir.

1 With your back to the church, turn left along the main road, away from the village. Opposite The Hall, turn right through a gate to visit the abbey ruins **A**. Return to and continue along the road. Bear right at a fork, and walk on downhill to the bridge.

2 Cross, go past the cottages and then turn immediately right through a gate. Bear right, uphill across the field. On the opposite bank is the old manor house **B**. Cross a stile, just below the far corner, into a wooded area. Where you emerge, cross the farm track, go over a stile and cut diagonally uphill, heading for a gap in the far hedge. Continue uphill to a gate in the top corner. Join a track running between hedges. Follow this as it bends left through a gate, then continue past the farm.

3 Where the track bends left uphill, turn right through the second gate into a field. Follow the hedge on your left to a gate into the next field. Turn left and aim between the two trees, then bear diagonally right downhill, to where the stream doglegs at the bottom of the field. Cross the stream and its fencing, emerging to the left of the fence running uphill in the field ahead. Continue around this field, keeping the fence to your right, to the second corner. Cross a fence and a small stream into a rough field. Keep straight ahead, over a fence. Keeping the hedge on your right, head for a gate onto a farm track.

4 Turn right, past the farm and through a gate. Bear right at the junction by the new farm buildings on your left. Continue on this track, ignoring turnings off, until you go through a gate and over a stream.

5 Turn right off the track and head uphill across the field. Follow the line of old fencing. Head through a narrow band of woodland towards the farm on the skyline. On the other side of the farm buildings, maintain your previous direction (south) along a farm track.

6 At the new barn, follow the track through gates and to the right. Continue as it winds uphill. At the top, admire the view **C** then continue ahead through fields, passing through two fence gaps. Head for the line of the fence running uphill on your left. At the gate in the corner, cross and turn right along a track beside the forestry. Keep straight ahead, to skirt another section of forestry. At its far corner, bear slightly right across the field to a larger area of forestry.

7 Go through a gate, into the trees **D**. At a fork, bear half right downhill and follow the main track. About 20 paces before another wide track joins from the right, turn left onto a faint, grassy path downhill. Turn almost immediately right onto a straight, tunnel-like path. At a junction of paths, continue walking straight ahead to a step stile into an open field. Cross the field, downhill to the footbridge. Turn right after the bridge and left after the gate to follow the fence to a gate into the lane. Turn right along the lane to return to the Happy Union Inn.

1644. All that is left now are the crumbling outlines of the nave walls, columns and altar steps.

The grassy nave is supposedly the last resting place of the headless body of Llywelyn ap Gruffudd, Prince of Wales, who was slain at Irfon Bridge by an English horseman, following his unsuccessful rebellion against Edward I in 1282.

ABIDING MEMORY

Llywelyn's head was cut off and sent to Edward. Mounted on an iron pole and crowned with ivy leaves, it decorated the Tower of London for 15 years. Llywelyn is not forgotten; fresh flowers are regularly placed on a stone memorial slab, unveiled in 1978 by the Arch Druid of Wales.

The route crosses Clywedog Brook, which once fed the abbey's mills and supplied the fishpond in the valley below. During the early

◀*Dyfaenor was built in 1680, using stone from the abbey, which had been destroyed by Cromwell's men in 1644.*

▼*What little remains of the stone-built abbey, including the nave walls here, is slowly being reclaimed by nature.*

years of the order, monks abstained from eating meat, and fish played an important part in their diet.

The old manor house, Dyfaenor **B**, stands on rising ground across the brook. It was built from the abbey's stones in 1680 in a Germanesque style. Three tall storeys surround a 14th-century staircase, which itself may have originated in the abbey. The windows were bricked up in 1777 to avoid payment of the much-hated Window Tax.

The path zigzags through rough open fields and across moors of hardy grasses, sedges and moss that are patrolled by ravens, buzzards and the magnificently powerful peregrine. Skylarks, meadow pipits, golden plovers, dunlin and snipe

▼*The route crosses fields bordered by woodland on its way towards a bare hill, the highest point of the walk.*

◄*The delightful and unusual pub sign outside The Happy Union Inn.*

Willow warblers, whinchats and redpolls are slowly being squeezed out by the gloom, though the tree tops are alive with siskins, crossbills and goldcrests. In the dark corridors between the trees, the heady smell of resin combines with the deep silence to create a claustrophobic yet curiously intoxicating effect.

TRANQUIL SCENE

As you leave the woods and break through again into daylight, the village, laid out before you beyond the brook, presents a picture of lasting serenity. A path takes you back down to The Happy Union Inn, whose sign depicts a portly Welshman, a leek in his hat, eating his meal astride a docile goat.

With his glass in one hand and his knife in the other, its subject appears the embodiment of bliss — even the goat looks content!

also live on these large, wild, upland tracts, where fist-sized mushrooms can be found in the autumn.

There is a breath-taking view **C** from the highest plateau. The Cambrian Mountains are to the north, and the Black Mountains to the south-east, while the distant, brooding heights of the Brecon Beacons fill the southern horizon.

The path winds on into forestry **D**, where conifers cover a huge area.

Sheep Country

The Cistercians were dynamic improvers of agricultural land. It was they who introduced sheep to the remote hill land of south and central Wales; several well known British breeds originated in Powys.

Apart from yielding meat, wool, skins, milk and tallow, sheep were essential soil improvers in the Middle Ages. Free-ranging on the hills in the daylight hours, at night they were driven down onto arable land to manure impoverished areas.

Sheep's milk cheese was savoured in the remote hamlets of Powys, and was readily available until about the end of World War II, its uniquely rich

texture and creamy flavour quite unlike cow's cheese. Mutton was the community's staple diet; huge pans of cawl (meat and vegetables) simmered in the farmhouse kitchen, while the shepherd whistled his dogs, driving flocks on their high summer pastures, or in their winter quarters in the sheltered fields of the valley.

Welsh sheep have evolved into a diverse range of hardy breeds, ideally adapted to this unyielding climate and rugged terrain. The most common breed is the Welsh Mountain sheep, a diminutive beast with an attractive tan face. A cross between white-faced Roman imports and the native

Soay, it has flourished in Wales for nearly 2,000 years.

Scottish settlers first introduced the Brecknock Cheviot to Wales in 1820. This breed thrives on the sandstone slopes of the Brecons, and its future is assured thanks to its strong wool, which is used to manufacture tweeds.

Hill Radnor ewes, which are larger and less hardy, produce one of the finest wools in Wales. The black-muzzled Kerry Hill, probably the largest breed, is found in the rolling green hills of central Powys. Its brilliant white wool can be dyed all shades and colours.

A white ewe with black lambs grazing on a Welsh hillside. It is quite common for certain breeds of white sheep to give birth to black lambs. These then become progressively paler as they grow older.

POWYS

◄A 17th-century mansion attached to the ruins of Hay-on-Wye's 13th-century castle is the backdrop to a sale of second-hand books. The rare allis shad (above) spawns in the River Wye.

Alongside a beautiful river and across a historic border

Hay-on-Wye has a colourful and turbulent history. A stretch of the River Wye forms the border between England and Wales, and the town suffered equally at the hands of English lords and enthusiastic Welsh patriots. Today, Hay is famous for housing the world's highest concentration of second-hand bookshops. The nearby village of Clyro also has a strong literary connection. Francis Kilvert (see box on page 124), the author of one of the finest diaries in the English language, was curate there.

The walk begins in Hay-on-Wye. This bustling market town, with its narrow lanes and picturesque inns, huddles beneath a castle **Ⓐ** that was built around 1200. Owain Glyndwr visited Hay around 1400, and marked the occasion by razing the castle, apart from its gateway and tower. These are now attached to an impressive Jacobean mansion. In 1971, Hay Castle was purchased by the self-appointed 'king' Richard Booth, who has been actively championing Hay's independence from Wales and England since around the end of the 1970s.

SECOND-HAND FIRST

The Old Fire Station **Ⓑ** in Castle Street was purchased by Booth in 1962, and established as Hay's first second-hand bookshop, thereby beginning a remarkable tradition. Today, there are 20 major bookshops in Hay, and many of these are open for 364 days of the year.

Down a narrow lane is St Mary's **Ⓒ**. The 13th-century church was enlarged and almost totally rebuilt in 1834. Inside, a crudely carved

block of stone is believed by some to represent 'Moll Walbee' — another name for Maud de Breos, the wife of the castle's builder — concerning whom there is some divergence of opinion. Gerald of Wales described her as an excellent woman; prudent, chaste and a marvellous house-keeper. Others stigmatized her as a sorceress, whose reputation as a baby-eating demon-worshipper persisted in Breconshire legend

◄The Old Fire Station was opened in 1962 as a second-hand bookshop, and proved to be the first of many in Hay.

FACT FILE

⚹ Hay-on-Wye, 18 miles (29km) west of Hereford, on the B4350

▭ Pathfinders 1015 (SO 04/14) and 1016 (SO 24/34), grid reference SO 228422

miles 0 1 2 3 4 5 6 7 8 9 10 miles
kms 0 1 2 3 4 5 6 7 8 9 10 11 12 13 14 15 kms

◷ Allow 4 hours

▭ Comfortable walking on country lanes, footpaths, farm tracks and riverside paths

P Car park at the start

T
I The Tourist Information Centre on Oxford Road has details of bus services, Tel. (01497) 820144

🍺🍴 Several pubs and cafés in Hay-on-Wye

🏰 The Kilvert Gallery in Clyro is open by appointment only. Tel. (01497) 820831

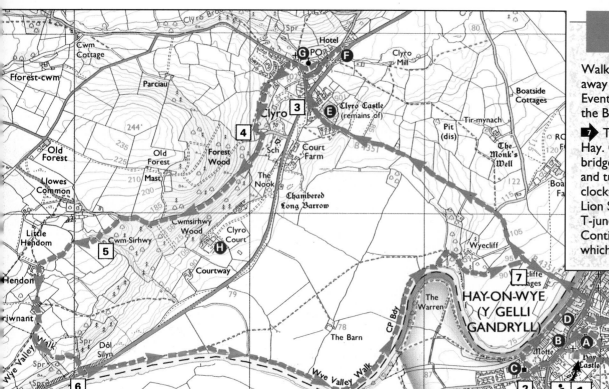

Walk, with Clyro Court **H** away to your left. Eventually, you come to the B4351.

➤ **7** Turn right towards Hay. Go over the river bridge to the T-junction and turn right. At the clocktower, turn left along Lion Street. At the T-junction, turn right. Continue on this road, which bends left away

HAY-ON-WYE – CLYRO

The walk begins from the car park next to the Tourist Information Centre in Oxford Road, Hay.

➤ **1** Turn right along Oxford Road, then first left into Oxford Terrace. Bear left into Castle Lane. Beyond the castle **A**, turn left into Castle Street. Pass the Old Fire Station **B** and continue into Church Street. Bear right alongside the Swan Hotel and follow the lane downhill, and over the bridge to reach St Mary's Church **C**.

➤ **2** Return towards the bridge and turn left onto a footpath alongside the church wall. Fork left, and go under a bridge to a T-junction. Turn right along the main path, between the River Wye and the old tramway **D**. At a bridge, go up and over it, then follow the road towards Clyro. Eventually, you pass a tree-covered mound on your right, the site of

Clyro Castle **E**, then come to a junction.

➤ **3** Cross diagonally right, and follow the road into Clyro village. Immediately beyond the post office is Ashbrook House **F**. Return past the post office and bear right into the churchyard. Continue past the church **G** into the lane, and turn right. Shortly after the lane bends left, turn left (uphill) onto a dirt lane. At the top, turn right over a step-stile by a gate. Cross the field, keeping the hedge line to your left. Go through a gate, and head towards the woods, with the hedge line on your right-hand side.

➤ **4** Go through a gate in the corner and turn left onto a farm track. Follow this down to a narrow lane and turn right. After approximately ¾ mile (1.2km), near the top of the hill and at the end of the woodland, turn left onto a dirt lane.

➤ **5** When the lane bends

left at the bottom, go straight ahead over a stile. Cross the field with the hedge to your right. Go through a gate and turn left to cross a field with the hedge on your left. Cross a stile beside a gate and continue towards Hendom farm. Go through two gates behind the farm buildings and turn left through a third gate. Cross two fields, keeping the fence on your right. Turn right through a gate in the corner, and cross the field with the hedge to your left, to Briwnant farm. Turn right, then left through the double gates between the barns. Go left along the farm track in front of the house. Go through a gate and pick up an old farm track between a double hedge. Continue downhill until you reach a gate onto a road.

➤ **6** Turn left. Immediately after a lay-by on your right, turn right, down to the river. Follow the waymarked Wye Valley

from the town. Cross a bridge, then turn right, signposted 'Cusop'.

➤ **8** Immediately beyond the de-restriction signs, turn left into a narrow lane signposted to St Mary's Church **J**. Leave the churchyard via the lychgate. Go straight ahead down the narrow lane to the T-junction and turn right. Immediately after a house on your left named Rosedale, turn left down a narrow lane. Cross a footbridge to join a narrow tarmac path. Go through a kissing-gate and cross a field; head for a kissing-gate in the wall opposite. Cross a field, keeping the fence to your left, go through a kissing-gate and cross fields to the car park at the start.

for over seven centuries.

You leave the town along a riverside path, its shrub- and ivy-covered banks brightened by pink splashes of Himalayan balsam. On the right is the line of the old tramway ⓓ from Brecon to Hay, which was constructed in 1816 to transport coal, corn and lime. Traffic was entirely horse-drawn, with each animal pulling six trams. Passengers were charged a penny a mile.

TOWERING SITE

The road leads across the river towards Clyro, and passes the site of a Norman motte and bailey castle ⓔ, which towers over the entrance to the village. Its guardians would have had an uninterrupted view to the Wye Valley. Kilvert wrote of his regret that the trees on the mound had been felled; now, they have grown back again, a dense tangle of oak, rowan and bramble.

A little further on is Ashbrook House ⓕ, Kilvert's lodgings from 1865 to 1872. It was here that he began writing his remarkable diary. Today, the house is sometimes used as a gallery to exhibit the work of local painters, sculptors and potters; otherwise it is open to the public by appointment only.

KILVERT'S CHURCH

Overlooking the house is the 12th-century Church of St Michael and All Angels ⓖ, rebuilt in 1853. On the north aisle wall of the austere building is a memorial tablet to Francis Kilvert; while the grassy churchyard contains the graves of many of the people of whom he wrote with such

▲ *View from the bridge as the route heads out of Hay over the River Wye. From here, a road leads to Clyro, and the Church of St Michael and All Angels (left) where Francis Kilvert was curate.*

warmth and humanity.

A twisting lane leads uphill away from the village, and the view opens out into a wide panorama. To the north are the rolling green hills of old Radnorshire, to the south and west are the mist-shrouded Black Mountains, and away to the east lies the fertile farmland of Herefordshire. The scene is little-changed since it was described by Kilvert in March 1871:

'An intense glare of primrose light streamed from the west,

◀ *As you return from Clyro, there are fine views of the Wye Valley, with its patchwork of fields. Near the river (above), where swans swim, molehills reveal the unseen presence of moles.*

deepening into rose and crimson. There was not a flake of snow anywhere but on the mountains and they stood up, the great white range rising high into the blue sky, while all the rest of the world at their feet lay ruddy rosy brown.'

You return along the banks of the Wye, an exceptionally clean and beautiful river. In summer, the tree-fringed valley is alive with insects and the birds that prey on them.

▲*Hay-on-Wye's interesting and historic buildings are framed by a magnificent backdrop of hills.*

Dominating the left bank is Clyro Court ➊, a modern reconstruction of an Elizabethan mansion that was once owned by the Baskervilles. It is said that Sir Arthur Conan Doyle visited the house; no doubt he saw the Baskerville coat of arms, which is surmounted by a vicious dog's head, and heard stories of the phantom hound that traditionally haunts nearby Hergest Court.

The route returns to Hay, then crosses into Herefordshire. In summer, the narrow lanes are overhung by mature, butterfly-haunted hedgerows. You pass through the peaceful village of Cusop and come to St Mary's Church ➋. In each corner of the graveyard is an ancient yew. These trees were recorded in the *Domesday Book*, and are thought to be over 2,000 years old.

The Curate of Clyro

Robert Francis Kilvert was 25 when he became curate of the small parish of Clyro in 1865. In 1870, he began keeping a diary, a unique personal record of life in and around the village. Although he reveals relatively little of himself in the diaries, his prose and poetry are the work of a warm-hearted idealist with a deep-rooted love of the countryside. Kilvert was also inspired by the peasantry, who lived, often in abject poverty, in tiny, isolated farmhouses and hovels in the hills. He shared their joys and sorrows with a sincere and passionate affection.

Kilvert's own poverty delayed his marriage until August 1879, when he took Elizabeth Rowland to be his wife. They honeymooned in York, Durham and Scotland, and returned to Wales in the highest of spirits. A few days later, he died of peritonitis.

Kilvert's niece, Mrs Essex Hope, inherited 22 notebooks. She gave away three volumes, and extracts from two of these were published between 1938 and 1940. There were plans to put the contents of all of the notebooks into print, but, some time before 1958, Mrs Hope destroyed her 19. She never explained why. Those enchanted by Kilvert's Diary can only hope that the one remaining volume may some day come to light.

Ashbrook House in Clyro was where Francis Kilvert began writing his now-famous diary.

SUSPENDED SENTENCE

The church is most famous for being the burial place of one Katherine Mary Armstrong, who lies in an unmarked grave. She was the victim of an infamous murder in the 1920s, when she was poisoned by her husband, Major Herbert Rowse Armstrong, who became the only solicitor ever to hang. Overlooking the field on the way back to Hay is a tall, balconied house, once known as Mayfield, where the mild-mannered Major Armstrong administered the fatal dose of arsenic.

INDEX

PICTURE CREDITS